D0097351

PHP

PHRASEBOOK

ESSENTIAL CODE AND COMMANDS

Christian Wenz

DEVELOPER'S
LIBRARY

Sams Publishing, 800 East 96th Street, Indianapolis, Indiana 46240 USA

PHP Phrasebook

International Standard Book Number: 0-672-32817-8

Library of Congress Catalog Card Number: 2005902706

Printed in the United States of America

First Printing: *September 2005*

08 07 06   4 3

Trademarks

All terms mentioned in this book that are known to be trademarks or service marks have been appropriately capitalized. Sams Publishing cannot attest to the accuracy of this information. Use of a term in this book should not be regarded as affecting the validity of any trademark or service mark.

Warning and Disclaimer

Every effort has been made to make this book as complete and as accurate as possible, but no warranty or fitness is implied. The information provided is on an "as is" basis. The author and the publisher shall have neither liability nor responsibility to any person or entity with respect to any loss or damages arising from the information contained in this book.

Bulk Purchases/Corporate Sales

Sams Publishing offers excellent discounts on this book when ordered in quantity for bulk purchases or special sales. For more information, please contact

U.S. Corporate and Government Sales
1-800-382-3419
corpsales@pearsontechgroup.com

For sales outside of the U.S., please contact

International Sales
international@pearsoned.com

Acquisitions Editor Shelley Johnston	**Copy Editor** Karen Annett	**Publishing Coordinator** Vanessa Evans
Development Editor Damon Jordan	**Indexer** John Sleeva	**Book Designer** Gary Adair
Managing Editor Charlotte Clapp	**Proofreader** Mindy Gutowski	**Page Layout** Toi Davis
Project Editor Andrew Beaster	**Technical Editor** Adam DeFields	

Table of Contents

Contents

Contents

About the Author

Christian Wenz is a professional phrasemonger, author, trainer, and consultant with a focus on web technologies. He has written or cowritten over four dozen books. He frequently contributes articles to renowned IT magazines and speaks at conferences around the globe. Christian contributes to several PHP packages in the PEAR repository and also maintains one Perl CPAN module. He holds a degree ("Diplom") in Computer Sciences from Technical University of Munich and lives and works in Munich, Germany. He also is Germany's very first Zend Certified Professional and founding principal at the PHP Security Consortium.

We Want to Hear from You!

As the reader of this book, *you* are our most important critic and commentator. We value your opinion and want to know what we're doing right, what we could do better, what areas you'd like to see us publish in, and any other words of wisdom you're willing to pass our way.

You can email or write me directly to let me know what you did or didn't like about this book—as well as what we can do to make our books stronger.

Please note that I cannot help you with technical problems related to the topic of this book, and that due to the high volume of mail I receive, I might not be able to reply to every message.

When you write, please be sure to include this book's title and author as well as your name and phone or email address. I will carefully review your comments and share them with the author and editors who worked on the book.

E-mail: opensource@samspublishing.com

Mail: Mark Taber
               Associate Publisher
               Sams Publishing
               800 East 96th Street
               Indianapolis, IN 46240 USA

Reader Services

For more information about this book or another Sams title, visit our website at www.samspublishing.com. Type the ISBN (excluding hyphens) or the title of a book in the Search field to find the page you're looking for.

Introduction

Some time ago, my favorite development editor, Damon Jordan, sent me an email and closed it with "Ich möchte eine Föhnwelle"—"I'd like a blow wave." Unfortunately, I didn't know what either a Föhnwelle or a blow wave is, so I declined. He then told me he had found this sentence in a German phrasebook he recently bought.

I was interested and had a look at some German phrasebooks. I think they are great tools to get around in a foreign country, although I personally think that some of the phrases offered just don't make sense. For instance, in one phrasebook, I found a series of pickup lines, including the ingenious "You have a beautiful personality," something that didn't work for me either in English, in German, or in any other language! Some coital guidance could also result in other problems— you either have to remember all the things to say while you are at it, or you have to hold the phrase-book in your free hand. And, finally, "Blow waves are as dead as a pet rock," just to use another phrase.

Anyway, we were discussing phrasebooks a bit, and Damon said that he wanted to do a book series on phrasebooks. He also mentioned that he would like to team up with his and my favorite acquisitions editor, Shelley Johnston, so I was in.

While working on a concept, we found some differences between a language phrasebook and an IT phrasebook. For instance, a language phrasebook just contrasts the same sentence in two languages. However, this is not always helpful. What if you want to change the phrase a bit, for instance if you want an en vogue blow wave (an oxymoron, one might say)?

So, we tried to create a concept that contains a lot of phrases, but all of them with good explanations so that it is easy to change the code and adapt it to one's needs. This, of course, makes the "foreign language" portions of a phrase a bit longer than the phrase itself, but we think that really helps when working with the book.

I also remember one famous Monty Python sketch in which someone uses a sabotaged dictionary, so that asking for directions results in getting roughed up. Therefore, it is vitally important to get a real explanation on what is going on within the phrase.

I then wrote a series concept and a sample chapter and now, only a few months later, you hold the first phrasebook in your hands, one of hopefully many.

Something I really hate about reading computer books is when code samples are hacked into the word processor, but never tested. To avoid this, every listing is also available for download at http:// php.phrasebook.org/, and the filename is part of the listing's caption for phrases longer than just a few lines. So every code does exist as a file and has actually been tested, unlike in some other books. Of course, it's an illusion that this book is 100% error-free, although we have taken several steps to come very close to that mark. Any errata, if known, will be posted to that site, too.

Another thing I really dislike with some books is that they tend to be very OS-dependent, which is really unnecessary for PHP. Some books were obviously only tested under Windows, some others only under Linux, but it is possible to make code relatively platform-independent. We have invested a lot of effort in testing the code from this book on many server platforms, including Linux, Windows, Mac OS X, and Solaris. Therefore, the screenshots in this book are also taken from those platforms, so you will find a healthy mixture of systems (and browsers). Ideology can be expressed with many phrases, but you won't find any of them in this book. If, however, something does only run on certain platforms (or PHP versions), it is noted in the text. Another phrase I promise you will not find in this book is anything that looks like foo, bar, baz, or any other proofs of very little imagination.

Of course, it is easy to find missing phrases in this book—PHP offers so much functionality that it is impossible to cover every aspect. Therefore, we had to select certain topics of interest—stuff that is relevant in a PHP programmer's everyday work. If you think, however, that something has really been overlooked, please let me know—but do also nominate something that should then be removed from upcoming editions of this book to make room for the new phrase(s). I am looking forward to hearing your feedback.

And now, to quote once more a phrasebook: "Bist du soweit? Da boxt der Papst"—"Are you ready? It's all happening there" (but literally: "There boxes the pope").

Your personal phrasemonger,

Christian Wenz

Manipulating Strings

Of all data types PHP supports, strings are probably the ones most often used. One of the reasons for this is that, at some point, a string representation of something is needed when sending out something to the client.

PHP offers a vast number of functions suitable for strings, almost 100. In addition, regular expressions come in handy when looking for certain patterns in strings. However, in real life only a fraction of these functions are actually used. Most of them deserve their loyal fan base; however, some underestimated functions should get more attention. The phrases in this chapter offer a good mix of both: standard applications and rather unusual, but very useful ways to work with strings.

Comparing Strings

```
strcmp($a, $b)
strcasecmp($a, $b)
```

Comparing strings seems like an easy task—use the == operator for implicit type conversion (so '1' == 1 returns true) or the === operator for type checking (so '1' === 1 returns false). However, the first method is rather flawed because the type conversions are not always turned into strings. For instance, 1 == '1twothree' returns true, too—both values are converted into integers. Therefore, === is the way to go.

However, PHP also offers functions that offer a bit more than just comparing strings and returning true or false. Instead, strcmp() returns a positive value when the string passed as the first parameter is greater than the second parameter, and a negative value when it is smaller. If both strings are equal, strcmp() returns 0. If no case sensitivity is required, strcasecmp() comes into play. It works as strcmp(); however, it does not distinguish between uppercase and lowercase letters.

```php
<?php
  $a = 'PHP';
  $b = 'php';
  echo 'strcmp(): ' . strcmp($a, $b) . '<br />';
  echo 'strcasecmp(): ' . strcasecmp($a, $b);
?>
```

Which outputs:

```
strcmp(): -1
strcasecmp(): 0
```

Comparing Strings (compare.php)

CHAPTER 1

These two functions can be used to sort arrays. More about custom array sorting can be found in Chapter 2, "Working with Arrays."

Checking Usernames and Passwords

When validating a username and a password (for example, in a script that backs an HTML login form), two things seem to form a de facto standard on the Web:

- The password is always case sensitive. It has to be provided exactly the same way it was set.

- The username, however, is not case sensitive.

Therefore, a username has to be compared without considering case sensitivity. This can be done either by using strcasecmp()—see the previous phrase—or by first converting both the provided password and the real password into lowercase letters (or uppercase letters). This is done by the functions strtolower() or strtoupper(). The preceding code shows an example, using strcmp()/strcasecmp() and also the compare operator ===.

```php
<?php
  $user = (isset($_GET['user'])) ? $_GET['user'] :
'';
  $pass = (isset($_GET['pass'])) ? $_GET['pass'] :
'';

  if (
    (strtolower($user) === 'damon' && $pass ===
'secret') ||
```

```
    (strtoupper($user) === 'SHELLEY' && $pass ===
'verysecret') ||
    (strcasecmp($user, 'Christian') == 0 &&
strcmp($pass, 'topsecret') == 0)
  ) {
    echo 'Login successful.';
  } else {
    echo 'Login failed.';
  }
?>
```

Validating Logins by Comparing Strings (comparelogin.php)

Depending on the data provided in the uniform resource locator (URL) of the call to the script, the login either fails or succeeds. For instance, the following URL successfully logs in the user (you have to change the servername portion):

```
http://servername/comparelogin.
php?user=cHRISTIAN&&pass=topsecret
```

On the other hand, the following login does fail:

```
http://servername/comparelogin.
php?user=Christian&&pass=TopSecret
```

NOTE
Of course, providing usernames and passwords via GET is a very bad idea; POST is preferred (see Chapter 4, "Interacting with Web Forms," for more details on form data). However, for testing purposes, this chapter's code uses GET.

Converting Strings into Hypertext Markup Language (HTML)

```
htmlspecialchars($input)
htmlentities($input)
```

A commonly used web attack is called Cross-Site Scripting (XSS). For example, a user enters some malicious data, such as JavaScript code, into a web form; the web page then at some point outputs this information verbatim, without proper escaping. Standard examples for this are web guest books or discussion forms. People enter text for others to see it.

```php
<?php
  $input = '<script>alert("I have a bad
Föhnwelle, ' .
          'therefore I crack
websites.");</script>';

  echo htmlspecialchars($input) . '<br />';
  echo htmlentities($input);
?>
```

Escaping Strings for HTML (htmlescape.php)

Here, it is important to remove certain HTML markup. To make a long story short: It is almost impossible to really catch all attempts to inject JavaScript into data. It's not only always done using the <script> tag, but also in other HTML elements, such as <img onerror="badCode()" />. Therefore, in most cases, all HTML must be removed.

MANIPULATING STRINGS

9

The easiest way to do so is to call `htmlspecialchars()`; this converts the string into HTML, including replacement of all < and > characters by `&lt;` and `&gt;`. Another option is to call `htmlentities()`. This uses HTML entities for characters, if available. The preceding code shows the differences between these two methods. The German ö (o umlaut) is not converted by `htmlspecialchars()`; however, `htmlentities()` replaces it by its entity `&ouml;`.

The use of `htmlspecialchars()` and `htmlentities()` just outputs what the user entered in the browser. So if the user entered HTML markup, this very markup is shown. So `htmlspecialchars()` and `htmlentities()` please the browser, but might not please the user.

> **NOTE**
>
> If you, however, want to prepare strings to be used within URLs, you have to use `urlencode()` to properly encode special characters such as the space character that can be used in URLs.

However, the function `strip_tags()` does completely get rid of all HTML elements. If you just want to keep some elements (for example, some limited formatting functionalities with `<b>` and `<i>` and `<br />` tags), you provide a list of allowed values in the second parameter for `strip_tags()`. The following script shows this; Figure 1.1 depicts its output. As you can see, all unwanted HTML tags have been removed; however, its contents are still there.

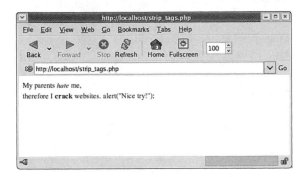

Figure 1.1 Some HTML tags were stripped, but not all.

```php
<?php
  $input = 'My parents <i>hate</i> me, <br />' .
    'therefore I <b>crack</b> websites. ' .
    '<script>alert("Nice try!");</script>' .
    '<img src="explicit.jpg" />';

  echo strip_tags($input, '<b><br><i>');
?>
```

Removing All HTML Tags (strip_tags.php)

Using Line Breaks

How can a line break be used within HTML? That's easy: with the `<br />` HTML element. However, what if there is data with \n or \r\n line breaks? Search and replace comes to mind; however, it is much easier to use a built-in PHP function: nl2br(). This parses a string and converts all line breaks to `<br />` elements, as the preceding script shows.

```php
<?php
  $input = "One\nTwo\r\nThree";
  echo nl2br($input);
?>
```

Outputs the HTML:

```
One<br />
Two<br />
Three
```

*Adding
 Elements at Every Line Break (nl2br.php)*

As you can see, the line breaks are still there, but the <br /> elements were added.

Encrypting Strings

```
$encpass = '$1$FK3.qn2.$Si5KhnprsRb.N.SEF4GMWO'
```

Passwords should never be stored verbatim in a database, but in an encrypted way. Some databases internally offer encryption; for all the others, PHP is there to help. The crypt() function encrypts a string using Data Encryption Standard (DES). This is a one-way encryption, so there is no way back. Also, subsequent calls to crypt() result in different results.

```php
<?php
  $pass = (isset($_GET['pass'])) ? $_GET['pass'] :
  '';
  $encpass = '$1$FK3.qn2.$Si5KhnprsRb.N.SEF4GMWO';

  if (crypt($pass, $encpass) === $encpass) {
    echo 'Login successful.';
```

```
  } else {
    echo 'Login failed.';
  }
?>
```

Checking Logins Using an Encrypted Password (crypt.php)

For instance, the string 'TopSecret' is encrypted into 1FK3.qn2.$Si5KhnprsRb.N.SEF4GMW0 (and also 1m61.1i2.$OplJ3EHwkIxycnyePplFz0 and $1$9S3.c/ 3.$5101Bm4v3cnBNOb1AECil., but this example sticks with the first one). Checking whether a value corresponds to a result from calling crypt() can be done by calling crypt() again: crypt($value, $encryptedValue) must return $encryptedValue.

The preceding script checks whether a password provided via the URL matches the previous result of crypt(). Calling this script with the GET parameter pass=TopSecret succeeds in logging in; all other passwords fail.

NOTE

To provide more details: The second parameter to crypt() is the salt (initialization value) for encrypting the data. You can also use a salt when encrypting the original password. However, you do have to make sure that the salt values are unique—otherwise, the encryption is not secure. Therefore, do not use a custom salt value and let PHP do the work.

Be also advised, though, that DES encryption can be cracked in about 24 hours, so it's not bulletproof anymore. A more recent alternative is Advanced Encryption Standard (AES).

Checksumming Strings

```
md5()
sha1()
```

Using crypt() with strings is similar to creating a
checksum of something: It can be easily determined
whether a string matches the checksum; however, it is
not (easily) possible to re-create the original string
from the checksum.

```php
<?php
  $pass = (isset($_GET['pass'])) ? $_GET['pass'] :
    '';

  $md5pass = '6958b43cb096e036f872d65d6a4dc01b';
  $sha1pass = '61c2feed11e0e53eb8e295ab8da78150be12
  f301';

  if (sha1($pass) === $sha1pass) {
    echo 'Login successful.';
  } else {
    echo 'Login failed.';
  }

// Alternatively, using MD5:
//  if (md5($pass) === $md5pass) {
//    echo 'Login successful.';
//  } else {
//    echo 'Login failed.';
//  }
?>
```

Checking Logins Using SHA1 and MD5 Hashes (checksum.php)

Two algorithms whose purpose is to do exactly this
checksumming are Secure Hash Algorithm 1 (SHA1)

CHAPTER 1

and Message Digest Algorithm 5 (MD5). They create such a checksum, or *hash*. The main difference between these two algorithms and the one used in DES/crypt() is: The SHA1 or MD5 checksum of a string is always the same, so it is very easy to verify data. As Figure 1.2 shows, even the PHP distributions have a MD5 checksum mentioned on the website to validate the downloads.

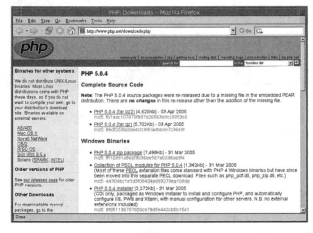

Figure 1.2   The PHP downloads page shows MD5 hashes of the PHP distributions.

Again, the goal is to validate a password the user provides using GET. The correct password is, once again, 'TopSecret' with the following hashes:

- 6958b43cb096e036f872d65d6a4dc01b is the MD5 hash

- 61c2feed11e0e53eb8e295ab8da78150be12f301 is the SHA1 hash

TIP

When calculating the MD5 or SHA1 hash of a file, no call to file_get_contents() or other file functions is required; PHP offers two functions that calculate the hashes of a file (and takes care of opening and reading in the file data):

- md5_file()
- sha1_file()

Extracting Substrings

substr()

The substr() function returns a part of a string. You provide a string and the position of the first character to be extracted (keep in mind that the first character has the index 0). From this character on, the rest of the string is returned. If you only want to return a part of it, provide the length in the third parameter. The preceding code shows substr() in action and extracts Prep from PHP: Hypertext Preprocessor.

```php
<?php
  $php = "PHP: Hypertext Preprocessor";
  echo substr($php, 15, 4); //returns "Prep"
?>
```

Extracting a Substring Using substr() (substr.php; excerpt)

> **TIP**
>
> If you want to count from the end of the string, use a negative value as the second parameter of substr():
>
>   echo substr($php, -12, 4);
>
> If you provide a negative value for the third parameter of substr(), for example -n, the last n characters are not part of the substring.
>
>   echo substr($php, -12, -8);
>
> All of these calls to substr() return Prep and are included into the complete code.

Protecting Email Addresses Using ASCII Codes

    protectMail('email@address.xy')

In the browser, you just see an email link; however, the underlying HTML markup is indecipherable:

```
<a href="&#109;&#97;&#105;&#108;&#116;&#111;&#58;
&#101;&#109;&#97;&#105;&#108;&#64;&#97;&#100;&#100;&#
114;&#101;&#115;&#115;&#46;&#120;&#121;">Send
mail</a>
```

```php
<?php
  function protectMail($s) {
    $result = '';
    $s = 'mailto:' . $s;
    for ($i = 0; $i < strlen($s); $i++) {
      $result .= '&#' . ord(substr($s, $i, 1)) .
        ';';
    }
    return $result;
  }
```

17

```
echo '<a href="' .
  protectMail('email@address.xy') .
  '">Send mail</a>';
?>
```

Protecting Email Addresses (protectMail.php)

However, take a look at Figure 1.3: The email address is decoded correctly by the web browser, as can be seen in the status bar.

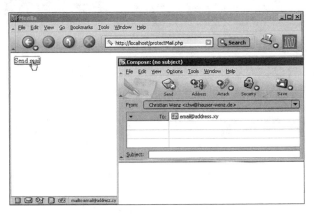

Figure 1.3   Machine beats man (when deciphering the email address).

Some special characters are difficult to use in strings because they are hard to enter using a keyboard. However, they all have an ASCII value. PHP offers two functions to deal with this:

- chr() converts the ASCII code into the corresponding character
- ord() returns the ASCII code for a character

CHAPTER 1

This can be used to protect email addresses, for instance. Because spammers are writing software to search for certain patterns (email adresses) on web pages, this might help keep spam low. The trick is to use HTML character codes for email addresses, making it much harder for spambots to find email data.

The preceding code takes an email address (in the format email@address.xy) as a parameter and returns mailto:email@address.xy—but converted into HTML entities. For instance, the m of mailto: has the ASCII code 109; therefore, $#109; stands for m. To do so, a for loop iterates through all characters in the string. To do so, the length of the string has to be determined, which can be done using strlen(). Then, a call to ord() calculates the ASCII code of each character, which is then used for the resulting HTML.

Of course, this does not offer a bulletproof protection; you might consider using alternative ways to obscure the email address, including a syntax such as email at address dot xy.

Printing Strings, Variables, and Expressions Simultaneously

Using double quotation marks, printing a mixture of strings and variables is easy to do. However, when you also want to use expressions such as function calls, the standard way is to use lots of string concatenations:

```
echo 'The length of the string is ' . strlen($s) .
  '!';
```

This is obviously getting rather complex when several expressions are involved.

A more convenient way is to use printf(). As parameters, you provide first a string with placeholders, and then the values for those placeholders. Table 1.1 shows which values are allowed for a placeholder.

Table 1.1   Placeholders for printf() and Related Functions

Placeholder	Description
%b	Integer value, binary representation is printed
%c	Integer value, ASCII representation is printed
%d	Integer value, signed decimal value is printed
%e	Decimal value in scientific notation (1.2e+34)
%f	Float value, printed with respect to the locale settings
%F	Float value, printed without respect to the locale settings
%o	Integer value, octal representation is printed
%s	String value
%u	Integer value, unsigned decimal value is printed
%x	Integer value, hexadecimal representation with lowercase letters is printed
%X	Integer value, hexadecimal representation with uppercase letters is printed

The following shows how printf() makes the code a bit easier to read:

```php
<?php
  $a = 'PHP';
  $b = 'php';
  printf('strcmp(): %d<br />strcasecmp(): %d',
    strcmp($a, $b), strcasecmp($a, $b));
?>
```

PHP also supports several functions related to printf():

- sprintf() works like printf(), but returns the string and does not print it.

- vprintf() works like printf(), however expects the values for the placeholders in the string to be in the form of an array.

- vsprintf() is a mixture of sprintf() and vprintf(): The placeholder values are provided in an array and the function returns the string but does not print it.

Scanning Formatted Strings

```
sscanf($date, '%d/%d/%d')
```

Another function related to printf() is sscanf(). This one parses a string and tries to match it with a pattern that contains placeholders. The $input string contains a date and is scanned using the string '%d-%d-%d' with several placeholders, as shown in the previous phrase. The function returns an array with all values for the matched placeholders. Then this array is passed to vprintf() to print it.

MANIPULATING STRINGS

```php
<?php
  $date = '02/01/06';
  $values = sscanf($date, '%d/%d/%d');
  vprintf('Month: %d; Day: %d; Year: %d.', $values);
?>
```

Scanning Formatted Strings (sscanf.php)

Alternatively, you can provide a list of variable names as additional parameters to sscanf(). Then the function writes the substrings that match the placeholders into these variables. The following code shows this:

```php
<?php
  $date = '02/01/06';
  $values = sscanf($date, '%d/%d/%d', $m, $d, $y);
  echo "Month: $m; Day: $d; Year: $y.";
?>
```

Scanning Formatted Strings (sscanf-alternative.php)

Getting Detailed Information About Variables

```
var_dump(false);
```

The values of variables can be sent to the client using print() or echo(); however, this is sometimes problematic. Take Booleans, for instance. echo(true) prints 1, but echo(false) prints nothing. A much better way is to use var_dump(), a function that also prints the type of the variable. Therefore, this code returns the string bool(false).

This also works for objects and arrays, making var_dump() a must-have option for developers who like to debug without a debugger.

> **NOTE**
>
> A function related to var_dump() is var_export(). It works similarly; however, there are two differences:
>
> - The return value of var_export() is PHP code; for instance, var_export(false) returns false.
>
> - If the second parameter provided to var_export() is the Boolean true, the function does not print anything, but returns a string.

Searching in Strings

```
if (strpos($string, $substring) === false) {
  echo 'No match found.';
} else {
  echo 'Match found.';
}
```

When looking for substrings in strings, strpos() is used (and its counterpart strrpos(), which searches from the end of the string). The tricky thing about this function is that it returns the index of the first occurrence of the substring, or false otherwise. That means that the preceding code snippet is incorrect.

The preceding code snippet is incorrect because if $string happens to start with $substring, strpos() returns 0, which evaluates to false. Therefore, a comparison using === or !== must be used to take the data type into account. The code at the beginning of this phrase shows how to correctly use strpos().

Understanding Regular Expressions

Regular expressions are, to put it simple, patterns that can be matched with strings. Two kinds of regular expressions are available in PHP—POSIX regular expressions and PHP regular expressions. The former can be installed when configuring PHP with the switch --with-regex. Windows users do not have to do this; the support for POSIX Regex is enabled by default.

The alternatives are Perl-compatible regular expressions (PCRE). PCRE are often said to be faster, and do offer more features. This functionality is enabled in PHP by default; however, if you compile PHP by yourself, you can deactivate PCRE using the switch --without-pcre-regex.

A pattern in a regular expression contains a string that can be searched for in a larger string. However, this can also be done (faster) using strpos(). The advantage of regular expressions is that some special features such as wildcards are available. Table 1.2 shows some special characters and their meaning.

Table 1.2   Special Characters in Regular Expressions

Special Character	Description	Example
^	Beginning of the string	^a means a string that starts with a

Table 1.2 Continues

Special Character	Description	Example
$	End of the string	a$ means a string that ends with a
?	0 or 1 times (refers to the previous character or expression)	ab? means a or ab
*	0 or more times (refers to the previous character or expression)	ab* means a or ab or abb or ...
+	1 or more times (refers to the previous character or expression)	ab+ means ab or abb or abbb or ...
[...]	Alternative characters	PHP[45] means PHP4 or PHP5
- (used within square brackets)	A sequence of values	PHP[3-5] means PHP3 or PHP4 or PHP5
^ (used within square brackets)	Matches anything but the following characters	[^A-C] means D or E or F or ...
		Alternative patterns	PHP4|PHP5 means PHP4 or PHP5
(...)	Defines a subpattern	(a)(b) means ab, but with two subpatterns (a and b)

Table 1.2   Continues

Special Character	Description	Example
.	Any character	. means a, b, c, 0, 1, 2, $, ^, ...
{min, max}	Minimum and maximum number of occurrences; if either min or max is omitted, it means 0 or infinite	a{1,3} means a, aa or aaa. a{,3} means empty string, a, aa, or aaa. a{1,} means a, aaa, aaa, ...
\	Escapes the following character	\. stands for .

> **TIP**
>
> The de facto standard reference for regular expressions is the title *Mastering Regular Expressions*, by Jeffrey E. F. Friedl. A bit dated, but a fun read.

Other special characters and expressions are available, for instance a character that refers to a digit. However, this differs between POSIX and PCRE, which in the example use [:digit:] and \d, respectively.

Using POSIX Regular Expressions

Searching for a match with POSIX regular expressions is done using the ereg() function. You provide a pattern, a string to search, and a variable name that receives the results as an array. The first element in this array is the complete match; the next elements are all matched subpatterns (defined in parentheses), from inner patterns to outer patterns, from left to right. The preceding code shows this, using the function phpversion() that returns the installed version of PHP. See Figure 1.4 for the output of this script when using PHP 5.0.4.

```php
<?php
  $string = 'This site runs on PHP ' . phpversion();
  ereg('PHP (([0-9])\.[0-9]\.[0-9]+)',
    $string, $matches);
  vprintf('Match: %s<br /> Version: %s; Major: %d.',
    $matches);
?>
```

Searching in Strings Using POSIX Regex (ereg.php)

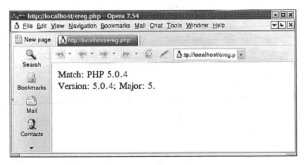

Figure 1.4 Splitting the PHP version
using regular expressions.

The + symbol after the last [0-9] expression in this example takes care of PHP versions like 4.3.11. If you do not want the search to be case sensitive, append an i to the function name: eregi().

> **TIP**
> The return value of ereg() is a Boolean that can be used
> to find out whether there was a match:
> ```
> if (ereg($pattern, $string)) {
>    echo 'Match found.'
> }
> ```

Using Perl-Compatible Regular Expressions

```
preg_match('/php ((\d)\.\d\.\d+)/i', $string,
$matches)
```

Matching patterns in PCRE is done using
preg_match() if only one occurrence is searched for, or
preg_match_all() if multiple occurrences may exist.
The syntax is the same as for ereg(): first the pattern,
then the string, then the resulting array. However, the
way the pattern is provided is slightly different. You
need delimiters; most of the time slashes are used. After
the delimiter, you can provide further instructions.
Instruction g lets the search be done globally (for multiple matches), whereas instruction i deactivates case
sensitivity.

```php
<?php
  $string = 'This site runs on PHP ' . phpversion();
  preg_match('/php ((\d)\.\d\.\d+)/i',
    $string, $matches);
  vprintf('Match: %s<br /> Version: %s; Major: %d.',
    $matches);
?>
```

The function `preg_match_all()` works exactly the same; however, the resulting array is a multi-dimensional one. Each entry in this array is an array of matches as it would have been returned by `preg_match()`. The following code shows this.

```php
<?php
  $string = 'This site runs on PHP ' . phpversion();
  preg_match('/php ((\d)\.\d\.\d+)/i',
    $string, $matches);
  vprintf('Match: %s<br /> Version: %s; Major: %d.',
    $matches);
?>
```

Finding Multiple Matches in Strings Using PCRE (preg_match_all.php)

Finding Tags with Regular Expressions

`preg_match_all('/<.*?>/', $string, $matches)`

One of the advantages of PCRE or POSIX is that some special constructs are supported. For instance, usually regular expressions are matched greedily. Take, for instance, this regular expression:

`<.*>`

When trying to match this in the following string:

`<p>Sex, drugs and <b>PHP</b>.</p>`

what do you get? You get the complete string. Of course, the pattern also matches on `<p>`, but regular expressions try to match as much as possible. Therefore, you usually have to do a clumsy workaround, such as `<[^>]*>`. However, it can be done more easily. You can use the ? modifier after the * quantifier to activate nongreedy matching.

```php
<?php
  $string = '<p>Sex, drugs and <b>PHP</b>.</p>';
  preg_match_all('/<.*?>/', $string, $matches);
  foreach ($matches[0] as $match) {
    echo htmlspecialchars("$match ");
  }
?>
```

Which outputs:

`<p> <b> </b> </p>`

Finding All Tags Using Non-greedy PCRE (non-greedy.php)

Validating Mandatory Input

```php
function checkNotEmpty($s) {
  return (trim($s) !== '');
}
```

When validating form fields (see Chapter 4 for more about HTML forms), several checks can be done. However, you should test as little as possible. For instance, when recently trying to order concert tickets for a U.S. concert, I always failed because it expected a U.S. telephone number, which couldn't be provided.

The best check is to check whether there is any input at all. However, what is considered to be "any input"? If someone enters just whitespace (that is, space characters and other nontext characters), is the form field filled out correctly?

The best way is to use trim() before checking whether there is anything inside the variable or expression. The function trim() removes all kinds of whitespace characters, including the space character, horizontal and vertical tabs, carriage returns, and line feeds. If, after that, the string is not equal to an empty string, the (mandatory) field has been filled out.

> **NOTE**
>
> The file check.php contains sample calls and all following calls to validation functions in the file check.inc.php.

Validating Numbers (and Other Data Types)

To find out whether any data is a number (or can be converted into a number), PHP offers several possibilities. First, the following helper functions check the data type of a variable:

- is_array()—Checks for array
- is_bool()—Checks for Boolean
- is_float()—Checks for float
- is_int()—Checks for integer
- is_null()—Checks for null
- is_numeric()—Checks for integers and floats
- is_object()—Checks for object
- is_string()—Checks for string

It is to be noted, however, that the numeric functions—is_float(), is_int(), and is_numeric()—

also try to convert the data from their original type to the numeric type.

Another approach to convert data types is something borrowed from Java and other strongly typed C-style languages. Prefix the variable or expression with the desired data type in parentheses:

```
$numericVar = (int)$originalVar;
```

In this case, however, PHP really tries to convert at any cost. Therefore, (int)'3DoorsDown' returns 3, whereas is_numeric('3DoorsDown') returns false. On the other hand, (int)'ThreeDoorsDown' returns 0.

Generally, is_numeric() (and is_int()/is_float()) seems to be the better alternative, whereas (int) returns an integer value even for illegal input. So, it's really a matter of the specific application at hand which method to choose.

The following code offers the best of both worlds. A given input is checked whether it is numeric with is_numeric(), and if so, it is converted into an integer using (int). Adaptions to support other (numeric) data types are trivial.

```
function getIntValue($s) {
  if (!is_numeric($s)) {
    return false;
  } else {
    return (int)$s;
  }
}
```

Generating Integer Values (check.inc.php; excerpt)

Validating Email Addresses

Checking whether a string contains a valid email address is two things at once: very common and very complicated. The aforementioned book on regular expressions uses several pages to create a set of regular expressions to perform this task. If you are interested in this, take a look at http://examples.oreilly.com/regex/readme.html.

```php
function checkEmail($s) {
  $lastDot = strrpos($s, '.');
  $ampersat = strrpos($s, '@');
  $length = strlen($s);
  return !(
    $lastDot === false ||
    $ampersat === false ||
    $length === false ||
    $lastDot - $ampersat < 3 ||
    $length - $lastDot < 3
  );
}
```

Validating Email Addresses (check.inc.php; excerpt)

Validating email addresses is difficult because the rules for valid domain names differ drastically between countries. For instance, bn.com is valid, whereas bn.de is not (but db.de is). Also, did you know that username@[127.0.0.1] is a valid email address (if 127.0.0.1 is the IP address of the mail server)?

Therefore, the recommendation is to only check for the major elements of an email address: valid characters (an @ character) and a dot somewhere after that. It is impossible to be 100% sure with checking email addresses—if the test is too strict, the user just provides a fantasy email address. The only purpose of email checking is to provide assistance when an (unintentional) typo occurs.

Of course, this is also possible using regular expressions, but this is probably just slower. You should also be aware that the aforementioned code cannot detect every email address that is incorrect. Also watch out for the new international domains with special characters such as ä or é in it. Most regular expressions omit these, so you are much better off with the preceding code.

Search and Replace

```
POSIX:
  egreg_replace()
PCRE:
  preg_replace()
```

Searching within strings is one thing; replacing all occurrences with something else is completely different. Using regular expressions, this is relatively easy; you just have to know the respective function names:

- For POSIX, use `ereg_replace()` and `eregi_replace()`

- For PCRE, use `preg_replace()`

```
POSIX:
<?php
  $string = '02/01/06';
  echo ereg_replace(
    '([0-9][0-9]?)/([0-9][0-9]?)/([0-9][0-9]?)',
    '\\2/\\1/\\3',
    $string
  );
?>
```

```
PCRE:
<?php
  $string = '02/01/06';
  echo preg_replace(
    '#(\d{1,2})/(\d{1,2})/(\d{1,2})#',
    '$2/$1/$3',
    $string
  );
?>
```

Replacing Matches Using POSIX (ereg_replace.php) and PCRE (preg_replace.php)

Within the regular expression for the replace term, you can use references to subpatterns. The complete match is referred to by \0 in POSIX and $0 in PCRE. Then count parentheses from inside to outside, from left to right: The contents of the first parentheses are referenced by \1 or $1, the second parentheses are accessed using \2 or $2, and so on.

With this in mind, the replacement can be done. In the example, a U.S. date (month/day/year) is converted to a U.K. date (day/month/year).

TIP

The regular expression in the preceding code does not use the / delimiter for the regular expression because the regular expression itself contains slashes that would then need escaping. However, by choosing another delimiter (for example: #), the escaping of slashes can be avoided.

If you have a static pattern, without any quantifiers or special characters, using str_replace() is almost always faster. The parameter order for this is: first the string(s) to search for; then the replacement(s); and, finally, the string where the search and replace shall take place. You can provide strings or arrays of strings in the first two parameters. The following code removes all punctuation from the text.

```php
<?php
  $string = 'To be, or not to be; that\'s the
question?!';
  echo str_replace(
    array('.', ',', ':', ';', '!', '?'),
    '',
    $string
  );
?>
```

Replacing Without Regular Expressions (str_replace.php)

Working with Arrays

When simple variables are just not good enough, arrays come into play (or objects, but that's another topic). The array section in the PHP manual, available at http://php.net/array, lists approximately 80 functions that are helpful. Therefore, this book could be filled with array-related phrases alone. However, not all of these functions are really used often. Therefore, this chapter presents the most important problems you'll have to solve when working with arrays—and, of course, solutions for these problems.

There are two types of arrays. The names they are given differ sometimes, but usually arrays are distinguished between numerical arrays and associative arrays. The first type of array uses numerical keys, whereas the latter type can also use strings as keys.

Creating an array can be done in one of two ways:

- Using the `array()` function

    ```
    $a = array('I', 'II', 'III', 'IV');
    ```

- Successively adding values to an array using the variable name and square brackets

```
$a[] = 'I';
$a[] = 'II';
$a[] = 'III';
$a[] = 'IV';
```

When using associative arrays, the same two methods can be used; however, this time keys and values must be provided:

```
$a1 = array('one' => 'I', 'two' => 'II', 'three' =>
  'III', 'four' => 'IV');
$a2['one'] = 'I';
$a2['two'] = 'II';
$a2['three'] = 'III';
$a2['four'] = 'IV';
```

Arrays can also be nested, when an array element itself is an array:

```
$a = array(
  'Roman' =>
    array('one' => 'I', 'two' -> 'II', 'three' ->
      'III', 'four' => 'IV'),
  'Arabic' =>
    array('one' => '1', 'two' => '2', 'three' =>
      '3', 'four' => '4')
);
```

Now, the Arabic representation of the number four can be accessed using $a['Arabic']['four'].

Of course, arrays are not only created within a script, but can also come from other sources, including from HTML forms (see Chapter 4, "Interacting with Web Forms") and from cookies and sessions (see Chapter 5, "Remembering Users (Cookies and Sessions)"). But if the array is there, what's next? The following phrases give some pointers.

Accessing All Elements of Numerical Arrays

```
array('I', 'II', 'III', 'IV');
```

Looping through numerical arrays can most easily be done using foreach because in each iteration of the loop, the current element in the array is automatically written in a variable.

```php
<?php
  $a = array('I', 'II', 'III', 'IV');
  foreach ($a as $element) {
    echo htmlspecialchars($element) . '<br />';
  }
?>
```

Looping Through an Array with foreach (foreach-n.php)

Alternatively, a for loop can also be used. The first array element has the index 0; the number of array indices can be retrieved using the count() function.

```php
<?php
  $a = array('I', 'II', 'III', 'IV');
  for ($i = 0; $i < count($a); $i++) {
    echo htmlspecialchars($a[$i]) . '<br />';
  }
?>
```

Looping Through an Array with for (for-n.php)

Both ways are equally good (or bad); though, usually, using foreach is the much more convenient way. However, there is a third possibility: The PHP function

WORKING WITH ARRAYS

39

each() returns the current element in an array. The return value of each() is an array, in which you can access the value using the numerical index 1, or the string index 'value'. Using a while loop, the whole array can be traversed. The following code once again prints all elements in the array, this time using each().

```php
<?php
  $a = array('I', 'II', 'III', 'IV');
  while ($element = each($a)) {
    echo htmlspecialchars($element['value']) .
      '<br />'; //or: $element[1]
  }
?>
```

Looping Through an Array with each() (each-n.php)

The output of the three listings is always the same, of course.

Accessing All Elements of Associative Arrays

foreach ($array as $key => $value) {

When using an associative array and wanting to access all data in it, the keys are also of relevance. For this, the foreach loop must also provide a variable name for the element's key, not only for its value.

```php
<?php
  foreach ($array as $key => $value) = array('one'
    => 'I', 'two' => 'II', 'three' => 'III', 'four'
    => 'IV');
```

```
  foreach ($array as $key => $value) {
    echo htmlspecialchars("$key: $value") . '<br
/>';
  }
?>
```

Looping Through an Associative Array with foreach (foreach-a.php)

Using count() is possible: count() returns the number of values in the array, not the number of elements. Looping through all array elements with for is not feasible. However, the combination of each() and while can be used, as can be seen in the following code. The important point is that the key name can be retrieved either using the index 0 or the string index 'key'.

```
<?php
  $a = array('one' => 'I', 'two' => 'II', 'three' =>
    'III', 'four' => 'IV');
  while ($element = each($a)) {
    echo htmlspecialchars($element['key'] . ': ' .
      $element['value']) . '<br />';
    //or: $element[0] / $element[1]
  }
?>
```

Looping Through an Array with each() (each-a.php)

Accessing All Array Elements in Nested Arrays

```
print_r($a);
```

Nested arrays can be printed really easily by using print_r(). Take a look at the output of the listing in Figure 2.1.

```
<pre>
<?php
  $a = array(
    'Roman' =>
      array('one' => 'I', 'two' => 'II', 'three' =>
        'III', 'four' => 'IV'),
    'Arabic' =>
      array('one' => '1', 'two' => '2', 'three' =>
        '3', 'four' => '4')
  );
  print_r($a);
?>
</pre>
```

Printing a nested array with print_r() (print_r.php)

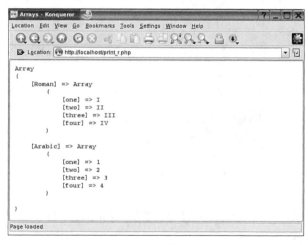

Figure 2.1 Printing array contents with print_r().

However, the output of the preceding code is hardly usable for more than debugging purposes (see Figure 2.1). Therefore, a clever way to access all data must be found. A recursive function is a reasonable way to achieve this. In this, all elements of an array are printed out; the whole output is indented using the HTML element `<blockquote>`. If, however, the array element's value is an array itself, the function calls itself recursively, which leads to an additional level of indention. Whether something is an array can be determined using the PHP function `is_array()`. Using this, the following code can be assembled. See Figure 2.2 for the result.

```php
<?php
  function printNestedArray($a) {
    echo '<blockquote>';
    foreach ($a as $key => $value) {
      echo htmlspecialchars("$key: ");
      if (is_array($value)) {
        printNestedArray($value);
      } else {
        echo htmlspecialchars($value) . '<br />';
      }
    }
    echo '</blockquote>';
  }
```

WORKING WITH ARRAYS

```
$arr = array(
    'Roman' =>
        array('one' => 'I', 'two' => 'II', 'three' =>
        'III', 'four' => 'IV'),
    'Arabic' =>
        array('one' => '1', 'two' => '2', 'three' =>
        '3', 'four' => '4')
);

printNestedArray($arr);
?>
```

Printing a Nested Array Using a Recursive Function
(printNestedArray.php)

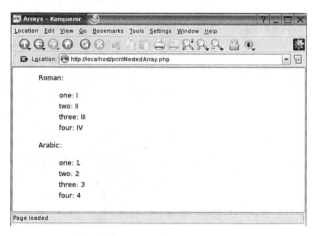

Figure 2.2 Printing array contents
using a recursive function.

Turning an Array into Variables

```
while (list($key, $value) = each($a))
```

Whenever each() is used, the use of list() is a good idea. Within list(), you provide variable names for all values with numerical indices in the array that is returned by each(). This makes while/each() loops even easier to use, as the code shows. Within the parentheses, the variable names are provided.

```php
<?php
  $a = array('one' => 'I', 'two' => 'II', 'three' =>
    'III', 'four' => 'IV');
  while (list($key, $value) = each($a))  {
    echo htmlspecialchars("$key: $value") . '<br
/>';
  }
?>
```

Looping Through an Array with list() and each() (each-list.php)

> **TIP**
>
> If you are only interested in either the key or the value of the array, you can remove one of the two variables; just make sure that you keep the comma.
>
> ```php
> while (list(, $value) = each($a)) {
>   echo htmlspecialchars("$value") .
>     '<br />';
> }
> ```

Converting Strings to Arrays

```php
$a = explode(',', $csvdata);
```

Sometimes, arrays are not used to store information; instead, a string is used. The single values are all within the string, but are separated by a special character. One example for this is the comma separated values (CSV) format.

```php
<?php
  $csvdata = 'Sams Publishing,800 East 96th
Street,Indianapolis,Indiana,46240';
  $a = explode(',', $csvdata);
  $info = print_r($a, true);
  echo "<pre>$info</pre>";
?>
```

Turning a String into an Array (explode.php)

The PHP function `explode()` creates an array out of these values; you just have to provide the character(s) at which the string needs to be split. The browser then shows this output:

```
Array
(
    [0] => Sams Publishing
    [1] => 800 East 96th Street
    [2] => Indianapolis
    [3] => Indiana
    [4] => 46240
)
```

Converting Arrays to Strings

```php
$address = implode('<br />', $data);
```

The way back (that is, making a string representation out of the elements in an array) can be done using `implode()`. Again, two parameters are required: the separation elements, then the array. The order is quite unusual, yet important.

So, PHP joins the elements of the array, using the `<br />` HTML element. Therefore, in the browser, each array's elements stay at its own line.

```php
<?php
  $data = array(
    'Sams Publishing',
    '800 East 96th Street',
    'Indianapolis',
    'Indiana',
    '46240'
  );
  $address = implode('<br />', $data);
  echo $address;
?>
```

Turning an Array into a String (implode.php)

Sorting Arrays Alphabetically

```
sort($a, SORT_NUMERIC);
sort($a, SORT_STRING);
```

Numerical arrays can be sorted rather easily by using
sort(). However, a problem exists if the array contains
both numerical and string values (for instance, "2" >
"10" but 2 < 10). Therefore, the sorting can be
tweaked so that a special data type is used for comparing elements when sorting:

- SORT_NUMERIC sorts elements as numbers

- SORT_REGULAR sorts elements according to their data
  type (standard behavior)

- SORT_STRING sorts elements as strings

```
<pre>
<?php
  $a = array('4', 31, '222', 1345);
  sort($a, SORT_NUMERIC);
```

```
  print_r($a);
  sort($a, SORT_STRING);
  print_r($a);
?>
</pre>
```

Sorting an Array (sort.php)

Here is the output of the preceding listing:

```
Array
(
    [0] => 4
    [1] => 31
    [2] => 222
    [3] => 1345
)
Array
(
    [0] => 1345
    [1] => 222
    [2] => 31
    [3] => 4
)
```

NOTE

If you want to sort the elements of the array in reverse order, use rsort() (r for reverse). The same optional second parameters are allowed that can be used with sort().

Sorting Associative Arrays Alphabetically

```
ksort($a);
asort($a);
```

Sorting associative arrays can be done in one of several ways:

- Sort by keys, leave key-value association intact: Use ksort().

- Sort by keys in reverse order, leave key-value association intact: Use krsort().

- Sort by values, leave key-value association intact: Use asort().

- Sort by values in reverse order, leave key-value association intact: Use arsort().

```
<pre>
<?php
  $a = array('one' => 'I', 'two' => 'II', 'three' =>
  'III', 'four' => 'IV');
  ksort($a);
  print_r($a);
  asort($a);
  print_r($a);
?>
</pre>
```

Sorting an Associative Array (sort_a.php)

The preceding code shows these functions in action; Figure 2.3 shows the result.

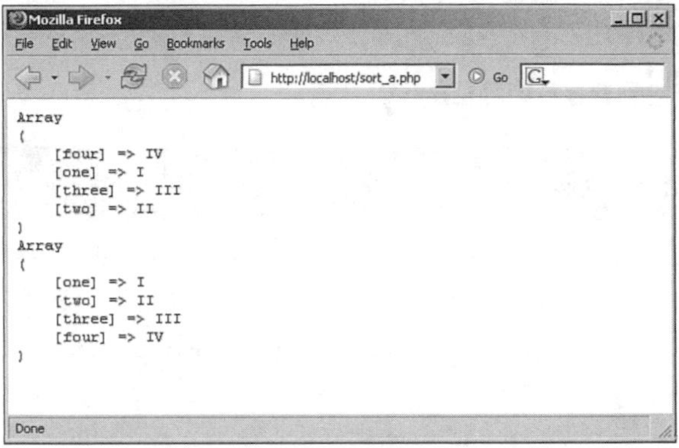

Sorting Nested Arrays

Figure 2.3   Sorting associative arrays.

NOTE

Trying to use sort() or rsort() with associative arrays
works—but the keys are then all lost.

Sorting Nested Arrays

```
function sortNestedArray(&$a) {
  sort($a);
  for ($i = 0; $i < count($a); $i++) {
    if (is_array($a[$i])) {
      sortNestedArray($a[$i]);
    }
  }
}
```

The standard sorting functions of PHP have to give up
when they work on nested arrays. However, if you use a
recursive function, you can code this in just a few lines.

The goal is to sort an array that is nested, but consists
only of numeric subarrays, so only numeric (and, therefore, useless) keys are used.

```
<pre>
<?php
  function sortNestedArray(&$a) {
    sort($a);
    for ($i = 0; $i < count($a); $i++) {
      if (is_array($a[$i])) {
        sortNestedArray($a[$i]);
      }
    }
  }

  $arr = array(
    'French',
    'Spanish',
    array('British English', 'American English'),
    'Portuguese',
    array('Schwitzerdütsch', 'Deutsch'),
    'Italian'
  );
  sortNestedArray($arr);
  print_r($arr);
?>
</pre>
```

Sorting a Nested Array Using a Recursive Function (sortNestedArray.php)

WORKING WITH ARRAYS

The idea is the following: Calling sort() does sort the array, but leaves out all subarrays. Therefore, for all elements that are arrays, the sorting function is called again, recursively. The preceding code shows this concept; Figure 2.4 shows the result for a sample array.

NOTE

The PHP function array_multisort() is an alternative way to sort arrays with more than one dimension; however, it has a rather unusual parameter order.

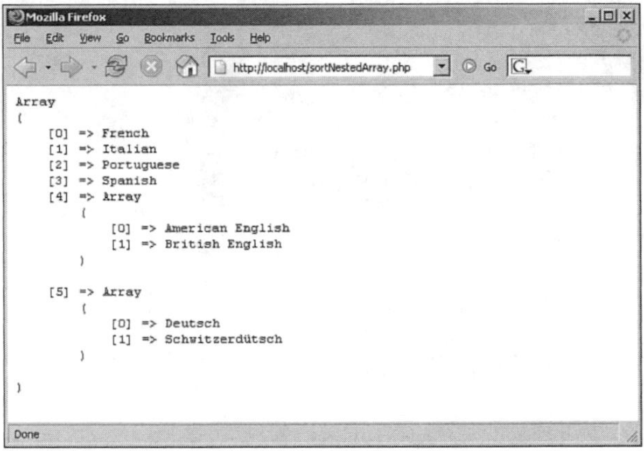

Figure 2.4 Sorting nested arrays.

Sorting Nested Associative Arrays

```
foreach ($a as $key => $value) {
  if (is_array($value)) {
    sortNestedArrayAssoc($value);
  }
}
```

If an associative nested array is to be sorted, two things have to be changed in comparison to the previous phrase that sorted a numeric (but nested) array. First, the array has to be sorted using ksort(), not sort(). Furthermore, the recursive sorting has to be applied to the right variable, the array element that itself is an array. Make sure that this is passed via reference, so that the changes are applied back to the value.

```
<pre>
<?php
  function sortNestedArrayAssoc($a) {
    ksort($a);
    foreach ($a as $key => $value) {
      if (is_array($value)) {
        sortNestedArrayAssoc($value);
      }
    }
  }

  $arr = array(
    'Roman' =>
      array('one' => 'I', 'two' => 'II', 'three' =>
        'III', 'four' => 'IV'),
    'Arabic' =>
      array('one' => '1', 'two' => '2', 'three' =>
        '3', 'four' => '4')
  );
  sortNestedArrayAssoc(&$arr);
  print_r($arr);
?>
</pre>
```

*Sorting a Nested Associative Array Using a Recursive Function
(sortNestedArrayAssoc.php)*

Figure 2.5 shows the result of the code at the beginning of this phrase.

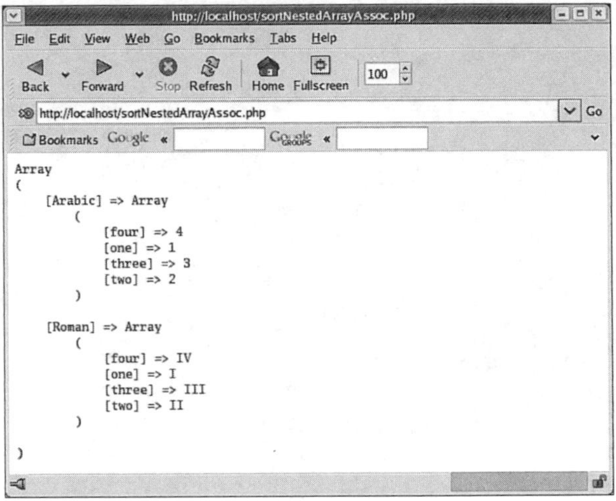

Figure 2.5 Sorting nested, associative arrays.

Sorting IP Addresses (as a Human Would)

```
natsort($a);
```

Sorting IP addresses with sort() does not really work because if sorting as strings, '100.200.300.400' is less than '50.60.70.80' (and not even a valid IP address, but this is not the point here). In addition, there are more than just digits within the string, so a numerical sorting does not work.

```php
<?php
  $a = array('100.200.300.400', '100.50.60.70',
    '100.8.9.0');
  natsort($a);
  echo implode(' < ', $a);
?>
```

Sorting IP Addresses Using a Natural Order String Comparison (natsort.php)

What is needed in this case is a so-called natural sorting, something that has been implemented by Martin Pool's Natural Order String Comparison project at http://sourcefrog.net/projects/natsort/. In PHP's natcasesort() function, this algorithm is used. According to the description, it sorts "as a human would." When case sensitivity is an issue, natsort() can be used. The preceding code shows the latter function.

NOTE

Internally, natsort() uses strnatcmp() (and natcasesort() uses strnatcasecmp()), which does a "natural" comparison of two strings. By calling this function a number of times, the array elements are brought into the correct order.

Sorting Anything

```php
function compare($a, $b) {
  return $a - $b;
}

$a = array(4, 1345, 31, 222);
usort($a, 'compare');
echo implode(' < ', $a);
```

WORKING WITH ARRAYS

If you do not want to limit yourself to the standard sorting functionality offered by PHP, you can write your own sorting algorithm. Internally, PHP uses the Quicksort algorithm to sort values in an array. For this to work, PHP has to know if two values are equal; in the latter case, PHP needs to find out which value is greater. So, to implement a custom sort, all that is required is a function that takes two parameters and returns:

- A negative value if the first parameter is smaller than the second parameter
- 0 if both parameters are equal
- A positive value if the second parameter is smaller than the first parameter

The name of this function must be passed to usort()—as a string! The rest of the work is done by PHP, as can be seen in the code. The comparison function used there is a very simple way to do a numeric sorting. By substracting the two values, the function returns the desired values: A positive number if the first parameter is larger than the second one, 0 if both parameters are equal, and a negative number otherwise.

> **NOTE**
>
> The Quicksort algorithm is one of the fastest algorithms to sort elements. When sorting n elements, it uses up to n? comparisons to do so; however, on average, only n log n comparisons are needed, making it really quick. Quicksort uses a divide-and-conquer strategy: It splits a problem into several smaller subproblems that can be solved recursively. More information about this algorithm can be found at http://en.wikipedia.org/wiki/Quicksort.

Sorting with Foreign Languages

Sorting works well, as long as only the standard ASCII characters are involved. However, as soon as special language characters come into play, the sorting yields an undesirable effect. For instance, calling sort() on an array with the values 'Frans', 'Frédéric', and 'Froni' puts 'Frédéric' last because the é character has a much larger charcode than o.

WORKING WITH ARRAYS

```php
<?php
  function compare($a, $b) {
    if ($a == $b) {
      return 0;
    } else {
      for ($i = 0; $i < min(strlen($a), strlen($b));
        $i++) {
        $cmp = compareChar(substr($a, $i, 1),
          substr($b, $i, 1));
        if ($cmp != 0) {
          return $cmp;
        }
      }
      return (strlen($a) > strlen($b)) ? 1 : 0;
    }
  }

  function compareChar($a, $b) {
    // ...
  }

  $a = array('Frédéric', 'Froni', 'Frans');
  usort($a, 'compare');
  echo implode(' < ', $a);
?>
```

*Sorting an Array with Language-Specific Characters
(languagesort.php; excerpt)*

For this special case, PHP offers no special sorting method; however, you can use strnatcmp()to emulate this behavior. The idea is to define a new order for some special characters; in the comparison function, you then use this to find out which character is "larger" and which is "smaller."

You first need a function that can sort single characters:

```php
function compareChar($a, $b) {
    $characters =
      'AÀÁÄBCÇDEÈÉFGHIÌÍJKLMNOÒÓÖPQRSTUÙÚÜVWXYZ';
    $characters .=
      'aàáäbcçdeèéfghiìíjklmnoòóöpqrstuùúüvwxyz';
    $pos_a = strpos($characters, $a);
    $pos_b = strpos($characters, $b);
    if ($pos_a === false) {
      if ($pos_b === false) {
        return 0;
      } else {
        return 1;
      }
    } elseif ($pos_b === false) {
      return -1;
    } else {
      return $pos_a - $pos_b;
    }
  }
```

Then, the main sorting function calls compareChar(), character for character, until a difference is found. If no difference is found, the longer string is considered to be the "greater" one. If both strings are identical, 0 is returned. The code at the beginning of this phrase shows the compare function. The result of this code is, as desired, Frans < Frédéric < Froni.

Applying an Effect to All Array Elements

```
$a = array_map('sanitize', $a);
```

Sometimes, data in an array has to be preprocessed before it can be used. In Chapter 4, you will see how data coming from the user via HTML forms can be sanitized before it is used. To do so, every array element must be touched.

```php
<?php
  function sanitize($s) {
    return htmlspecialchars($s);
  }

  $a = array('harmless', '<bad>', '>>click
here!<<');
  $a = array_map('sanitize', $a);
  echo implode(' ', $a);
?>
```

Applying htmlspecialchars() to All Elements of an Array (array_map.php)

However, it is not required that you do a cumbersome for/foreach/while loop; PHP offers built-in functionality for this. The first possibility is to use array_map(). This takes an array (second parameter) and submits every element in that array to a callback function (first parameter, as a string). At the end, the array is returned, with all of the elements replaced by the associated return values of the callback function.

In the preceding listing, all values in the array are converted into HTML using htmlspecialchars().

If, however, the array turns out to be a nested one, the tactic has to be changed a little. Then a recursive function can be used. If an array element is a string, it is HTML-encoded. If it's an array, the recursive function calls itself on that array. The following code implements this, and Figure 2.6 shows the result.

```php
<?php
  function sanitize_recursive($s) {
    if (is_array($s)) {
      return(array_map('sanitize_recursive', $s));
    } else {
      return htmlspecialchars($s);
    }
  }

  $a = array(
    'harmless' =>
      array('no', 'problem'),
    'harmful' =>
      array('<bad>', '--> <worse> <<-')
  );

  $a = sanitize_recursive($a);
  echo '<pre>' . print_r($a, true) . '</pre>';
?>
```

Recursively Applying htmlspecialchars() to All Elements of a Nested Array (array_map_recursive.php)

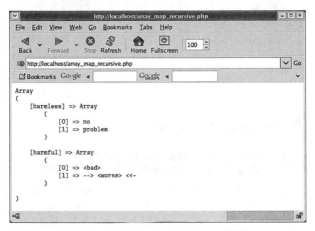

Figure 2.6 The nested arrays have been HTML-encoded.

Another function that behaves similarly is array_walk(). This one also applies a function to every element of an array; however, it also allows you to provide a parameter for this function call. In the following code, this is used to print out all elements of an array. A parameter is passed—a counter. Because it is passed by reference, increasing this counter by 1 within the function leads to a sequence of numbers.

```php
<?php
  function printElement($s, &$i) {
    printf('%d: %s<br />', $i,
      htmlspecialchars($s));
    $i++;
  }
  $i = 1;
  $a = array('one', 'two', 'three', 'four');
  $a = array_walk($a, 'printElement', $i);
?>
```

Printing Array Elements Using array_walk() and a Counter Passed by Reference (array_walk.php)

Running the preceding code shows the following:

```
0: one
1: two
2: three
3: four
```

Filtering Arrays

```
array_filter($values, 'checkMail'))
```

Imagine you get a bunch of values—from an HTML form, a file, or a database—and want to select which of these values are actually usable and which are not. You could again call for, foreach, or while and find out what is interesting, or you can let PHP do most of the work. In the latter case, get acquainted with the function array_filter(). This one takes two parameters—first, the array to be filtered and, second, a function name (as a string) that checks whether an array element is good. This validation function returns true upon success and false otherwise. The following is a very simplistic validation function for email addresses (see Chapter 1, "Manipulating Strings," for a discussion of this topic).

```php
<?php
function checkMail($s) {
  $ampersand = strpos($s, '@');
  $lastDot = strrpos($s, '.');
  return ($ampersand !== false &&
          $lastDot !== false &&
          $lastDot - $ampersand >= 3);
}
```

```
$values = array(
  'valid@email.tld',
  'invalid@email',
  'also@i.nvalid',
  'also@val.id'
);
echo implode(', ', array_filter($values,
  'checkMail'));
?>
```

Filtering Valid Email Addresses (array_filter.php)

Now, the code at the beginning of this phrase calls
array_filter(), so that only (syntactically) valid email
addresses are left.

As you would expect, the code just prints out the two
valid email addresses.

Getting Random Elements Out of Arrays

`array_rand($numbers, 6)`

With array_rand(), one or more random elements out
of an array are determined by random. This can, for
instance, be used to draw some lucky numbers. For
instance, the German lottery draws six numbers out of
49. The preceding code implements this drawing using
PHP and array_rand(); see Figure 2.7 for its output. The
first parameter for this function is the array; the second
(optional) one is the number of elements to be returned.

WORKING WITH ARRAYS

```php
<?php
  for ($i = 1; $i <= 49; $i++) {
    $numbers[] = $i;
  }
  echo implode(' ', array_rand($numbers, 6));
?>
```

Picking Random Elements Out of an Array (array_rand.php)

NOTE

If you do not want to pick random elements but want to randomize the order of elements in the array (for example, when shuffling a deck of cards), use the shuffle() function.

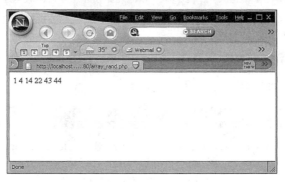

Figure 2.7 Lucky numbers with PHP.

Date and Time

Most of the time, the date and time functionalities of PHP 5 are used for printing out the current date and time—to pretend that the web page is up to date (you would be surprised how many larger websites actually use this). But apart from that, working with date and time in PHP offers many other possibilities, most of which you will find in this chapter.

First, though, it seems appropriate to have a look at the PHP function that is probably used the most for working with dates—date(). This function can take the current date (or an arbitrary one) and extract some information about it, for example, the day, whether it's a.m. or p.m., and what time it is according to the rather failed marketing stunt, "Swatch Internet Time." To do so, you call date() and provide a string as the first parameter. This string may now contain a list of formatting symbols that can be seen in Table 3.1 (the PHP manual carries a list with more examples at http://php.net/date). Each of these symbols is replaced by the associated date/time value.

Table 3.1   Formatting Symbols for date()

Symbol	Description
a	am or pm
A	AM or PM
B	Swatch Internet Time (between 000 and 999)
c	Date in ISO 8601 format
d	Day of month (from 01 to 31)
D	Day of week (from Mon to Sun)
F	Month (from January to December)
g	Hour (from 1 to 12)
G	Hour (from 0 to 23)
h	Hour (from 01 to 12)
H	Hour (from 00 to 23)
i	Minutes (from 00 to 59)
I	Whether date is in DST (1) or not (0)
j	Day of month (between 1 and 31)
l	Day of month (from Sunday to Saturday)
L	Whether date is in a leap year (1) or not (0)
m	Month (from 01 to 12)
M	Month (from Jan to Dec)
n	Month (from 1 to 12)
O	Difference to GMT (for example, +0100 for one hour ahead)
r	Date in RFC 2822 format
s	Seconds (from 00 to 59)
S	Ordinal suffix for the day of month (st, nr, td, th)
t	Number of days in the provided month (from 28 to 31)
T	Time zone of server (for example, CET)

Table 3.1   Continued

Symbol	Description
U	Epoche value (seconds since January 1st, 1970, Midnight GMT)
w	Day of week (from 0—Sunday, to 6—Saturday)
W	Week number (according to ISO 8601, from 1 to 53)
y	Year (two digits)
Y	Year (four digits)
z	Day of year (from 0 to 365)
Z	Time zone difference to UTC (in seconds)

NOTE

Almost all of the formatting symbols shown in Table 3.1 are available since PHP 3. There are only two exceptions: Using W for determining the week number of a date was added in PHP 4.1.0, and using c for retrieving the ISO 8601 representation for a date (for example, 2006-06-30T12:34:56+01:00) came in PHP 5.

The function date() is very powerful and offers a broad range of ways to use it. However, especially if you have localized content, you need some good phrases. In this chapter, you will find many of them.

PHP's date and time functions have their own section in the PHP manual. You can find more information about date() and friends at http://php.net/datetime.

DATE AND TIME

Using Text Within date()

```
date('\To\d\a\y \i\s \t\he jS \d\a\y of F')
```

Imagine you want to output the current date (or a specific date) and use custom strings in it. The code could look like a mess if you are trying it like this:

```php
<?php
  echo 'Today is the ' . date('jS') . ' day of the
    month ' . date('F');
?>
```

```php
<?php
  echo date('\To\d\a\y \i\s \t\he jS \d\a\y of F');
?>
```

Using Ordinary Characters in date() (date.php)

The output of this script is something like this, depending on the current date:

```
Today is the 3rd day of the month May
```

The behavior of date() is the following: All characters within the first parameter that bear a special meaning (for example, formatting symbols) get replaced by the appropriate values. All other characters, however, remain unchanged. If a character is escaped using the backslash character (\), it is returned verbatim. So, the code at the beginning of this phrase shows a new version of the code that only uses one call to date().

> **NOTE**
> If you are using double quotes instead of single quotes, you might get into trouble when escaping certain characters within date(). In the previous example, escaping the n would be done with \n, which (within double quotes) gets replaced by the newline character.

Automatically Localizing Dates

```
setlocale(LC_TIME, 'en_US');
echo strftime('In (American) English: %c<br />');
```

The PHP function strftime() formats a date/time value according to the sytem's locale, for example, to the web server's local settings. Generally, the language of the system is automatically used. However, this can be overridden using setlocale().

```php
<?php
  setlocale(LC_TIME, 'en_US');
  echo strftime('In (American) English: %c<br />');
  setlocale(LC_TIME, 'en_gb');
  echo strftime('In (British) English: %c<br />');
  setlocale(LC_TIME, 'de_DE');
  echo strftime('Auf Deutsch: %c<br />');
  setlocale(LC_TIME, 'fr_FR');
  echo strftime('En Français: %c');
?>
```

Localizing Dates Using strftime() (strftime.php)

The function strftime() expects a format string (as does date()) in which it accepts a large number of special symbols. Table 3.2 contains a full list.

Table 3.2 Formatting Symbols for strftime()

Symbol	Description
%a	Day of week (abbreviated)
%A	Day of week
%b or %h	Month (abbreviated)
%B	Month
%c	Date and time in standard format
%C	Century
%d	Day of month (from 01 to 31)
%D	Date in abbreviated format (mm/dd/yy)
%e	Day of month as a two-character string (from ' 1' to '31')
%g	Year according to the week number, two digits
%G	Year according to the week number, four digits
%H	Hour (from 00 to 23)
%I	Hour (from 01 to 12)
%j	Day of year (from 001 to 366)
%m	Month (from 01 to 12)
%M	Minute (from 00 to 59)
%n	Newline (\n)
%p	am or pm (or local equivalent)
%r	Time using a.m./p.m. notation
%R	Time using 24 hours notation
%S	Second (from 00 to 59)
%t	Tab (\t)
%T	Time in hh:ss:mm format
%u	Day of week (from 1—Monday—to 7—Sunday)

Table 3.2   Continued

Symbol	Description
%U	Week number (Rule: The first Sunday is the first day of the first week.)
%V	Week number (Rule: The first week in the year with at least four days counts as week number 1.)
%w	Day of week (from 0—Sunday to 6—Saturday)
%W	Week number (Rule: The first Monday is the first day of the first week.)
%x	Date in standard format (without the time)
%X	Time in standard format (without the date)
%y	Year (two digits)
%Y	Year (four digits)
%z or %Z	Time zone

Whenever it says *standard format* in Table 3.2, the formatting symbol gets replaced by the associated value according to the local setting. The preceding code changes the locale several times using `setlocale()` and then calls `strftime()`. Note the differences that can be seen in Figure 3.1. Also take a look at Figure 3.2, in which the same script was executed on a Windows machine. According to the documentation, most of `strftime()` also works on Windows, but on some configurations changing the locale just does not seem to work. Therefore, it is very important to test first whether the system supports localized dates.

DATE AND TIME

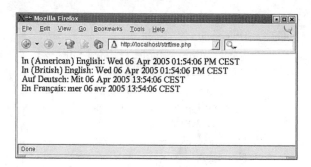

Figure 3.1   The current date in different locales.

Figure 3.2   This particular system does
not seem to support locales.

Manually Localizing Dates

If you cannot rely on setlocale(), yet want to use
localized date and time values, you have to do the
translations by yourself and store the results in an array.
Then, you can use date() to retrieve information
about a date. This serves as an index for your array.

```php
<?php
  $weekdays = array(
    'domingo', 'lunes', 'martes', 'miércoles',
    'jueves', 'viernes', 'sábado'
  );
  $months = array(
    'enero', 'febrero', 'marzo', 'abril',
    'mayo', 'junio', 'julio', 'agosto',
    'septiembre', 'octubre', 'noviembre',
       'diciembre'
  );
  $weekday = date('w');
  $month = date('n');
  echo $weekdays[$weekday] . date(', j ') .
    $months[$month - 1] . date(' Y');
?>
```

Localizing Dates Manually (localdate.php)

The preceding code does this for both the day of the month and the month itself. One array contains the Spanish weekdays; another one contains the month names.

Note that the value for the month is decreased by 1 because the array $months has no dummy element at position 0; therefore, month number one (January) has the index 0.

Using the Current Date the U.S./U.K./European Way

```php
<?php
  echo 'US format: ' . date('m/d/Y<b\r />');
  echo 'UK format: ' . date('d/m/Y<b\r />');
  echo 'German format: ' . date('d.m.Y<b\r />');
  echo 'International format: ' . date('Y-d-m');
?>
```

To give you a short and convenient reference, the preceding code contains several commonly used date formats. Depending on where you are, the order in which day, month, and year are used might vary:

- In the United States, it's (mostly) month, day, and year

- In the United Kingdom and the rest of Europe, it's (mostly) day, month, and year

- The international standard date notation starts with the year and continues with month and day

NOTE

The preceding code used a four-digit representation of the year because this is nonambiguous. In practice, however, two-digit years are also commonly used.

Formatting a Specific Date

```
echo 'Time stamp: ' . mktime(12, 0, 0, 1, 1, 2001);
```

All previous phrases in this chapter have used the current date and time. However, it is also possible to use any other arbitrary date and time value. For this, the relevant functions (especially date() and strftime()) accept a second parameter—a time stamp of the date to be analyzed. This time stamp is an integer value, the date and time in the so-called epoche format. This is the number of seconds that passed since January 1st, 1970, midnight GMT—the beginning of the UNIX epoche. The time stamp/epoche value of the current moment can be retrieved using time() or by calling date('U') (see Table 3.1).

If you want to use another date, `mktime()` comes into play. This function converts a date provided by year, month, day, hour, minute, and second into an epoche value. Probably the strangest thing about this function is the order in which these parameters are passed:

1. Hour
2. Minute
3. Second
4. Month
5. Day
6. Year

You can also provide an optional seventh parameter, regardless of whether it is Daylight Savings Time (DST). This is relevant close to the change from or to DST because that does not happen at the same time over the world.

The preceding code calculates the time stamp for noon on the first day of this millennium. Because there was no year 0, this was January 1st, 2001.

DATE AND TIME

> **NOTE**
>
> If you love collecting useless facts: On September 9, 2001, at precisely 3:46:40 a.m., the time stamp was 1,000,000,000. Therefore, `mktime(3, 46, 40, 9, 9, 2001)` returns 1000000000 (if your time zone is Central Europe).

Validating a Date

```
checkdate(2, 29, 2000)
```

When you get a date—for example, from the user using an HTML form—this data must be validated. This includes checking whether the month exists and if the month has enough days. If it's February, you might also want to find out whether it is a leap year.

```php
<?php
  echo '2000 was ' .
    (checkdate(2, 29, 2000) ? 'a' : 'no') .
    ' leap year.<br />';
  echo '2100 will be ' .
    (checkdate(2, 29, 2100) ? 'a' : 'no') .
    ' leap year.';
?>
```

Validating Date Information (checkdate.php)

But PHP would not be PHP if you really had to do this on your own. The function checkdate() validates a date; you provide the month, the day, and the year as parameters.

Calculating a Relative Date

```php
echo 'The license you have just bought is valid
  till ';
$expiry = time() + 30 * 24 * 60 * 60; //30 days)
echo strftime('%c', $expiry);
```

TIP

Why was 2000 a leap year, but 2100 not? The definition says: If a year is divisible by 4 and is either not divisible by 100 or is divisible by 400, it is a leap year and February has 29 days (this is because the Earth needs approximately 365.25 days to revolve around the sun). If you want to determine whether a given year is a leap year, this function comes in handy:

```
function isLeapYear($year) {
  return ($year % 4 == 0 &&
    ($year % 100 != 0 || $year % 400 == 0));
}
```

Sometimes, you have the task of calculating a date that is relative to the current date, for example, "30 days from now." Of course, you could put some real work into actually calculating this value, taking into account which day it is, whether it's a leap year, and whether DST is relevant.

Far easier is the use of an epoche time stamp. Take, for instance, the aforementioned task of finding a date that lies 30 days in the future. One day has 24 hours, one hour has 60 minutes, and one minute has 60 seconds. Therefore, to get the current time stamp (using `time()` or `date('U')`), you just need to add 30 * 24 * 60 * 60, and you have the time stamp of the desired date. This time stamp can then be used to set a cookie's expiry date or just to print out some information about this date.

Creating a Sortable Time Stamp

```
function timestamp($t = null) {
  if ($t == null) {
    $t = time();
  }
  return date('YmdHis', $t);
}
```

Sometimes, using date values with a database is not a clever thing. Different language versions of the database, its drivers, or the underlying operating system could cause some trouble when the regional date formats do not fit together.

```
<?php
  function timestamp($t = null) {
    if ($t == null) {
      $t = time();
    }
    return date('YmdHis', $t);
  }

  echo 'Time stamp: ' . timestamp(time());
?>
```

Converting a Date into a (Sortable) Time Stamp (timestamp.php)

A potential alternative is the use of time stamps. Several different formats are available, but most of them have the following structure: year-month-day-hours-minutes-seconds. Using this value order, the string representation of the date can be easily sorted, which allows using it in databases.

To create such a time stamp, just a special call to date() is required. In the preceding code, this is encapsulated in a function for easy reuse.

> **TIP**
> This format is also used by MySQL for the representation of its TIMESTAMP data type.

Converting a String into a Date

```
'Yesterday: ' . date('r', strtotime('Yesterday'))
```

Previously, you saw a numeric representation of a date—either a triplet of day, month, and year, or a time stamp value. This time, you can go the other way and convert a string representation of a date/time value into an epoche value or something else that is usable within PHP and its date/time functions.

```php
<?php
  echo 'Yesterday: ' . date('r',
    strtotime('Yesterday')) . '<br />';
  echo 'Today: ' . date('r', strtotime('Today')) .
    '<br />';
  echo 'Tomorrow: ' . date('r',
    strtotime('Tomorrow')) . '<br />';
  echo 'In one week: ' . date('r', strtotime('+1
    week')) . '<br />';
  echo 'One month before: ' . date('r', strtotime('-
    1 month')) . '<br />';
  echo 'Last Sunday: ' . date('r', strtotime('Last
    Sunday')) . '<br />';
  echo 'Next fantasy day: ' .
    var_export(@date('r', strtotime('Next fantasy
    day')), true);
?>
```

Converting a String into a Date (strtotime.php)

DATE AND TIME

The whole magic is put into the PHP function strtotime(). According to the documentation, it "parse[s] about any English textual date/time description into a UNIX time stamp." It sounds amazing, and it is amazing. The basis for this is the GNU date syntax; the code at the beginning of this phrase shows some examples for strtotime().

> **NOTE**
>
> At the time of this writing, strtotime() shows some strange behavior when a relative date is calculated and a change from or to DST is imminent. Also at the time of this writing, PHP's date/time functions are about be rewritten and amended.

Determining Sunrise and Sunset

```
date_sunrise(time(), SUNFUNCS_RET_STRING, 48, 11.5,
90, 1);
date_sunset(time(), SUNFUNCS_RET_STRING, 48, 11.5,
90, 1);
```

Depending on the current location and date, the times for sunrise and sunset can drastically vary. However, formulas exist for determining this value depending on latitude and longitude, and PHP has this functionality integrated into its core starting with PHP 5. All you are required to do is call date_sunrise() and date_sunset(). Both functions expect a number of parameters:

- A time stamp (epoche value) of the date for which to determine the sunrise/sunset

- The desired format for the return value: SUFUNCS_RET_DOUBLE returns the time as a float value (between 0 and 23.99), SUNFUNCS_RET_STRING returns it as a string (between 00:00 and 23:59), and SUNFUNCS_RET_TIMESTAMP returns an epoche value

- The latitude (Northern latitude; use negative values for a Southern latitude)

- The longitude (Eastern longitude; use negative values for a Western longitude)

- The zenith of the sunrise (in degrees)

- The offset (in hours) to Greenwich mean time (GMT)

So, the preceding code (in sun.php) calculates the sunrise and sunset for Munich, Germany, which resides at about 48° Northern latitude, 11° 30' Eastern longitude, for the current day. I checked it: It worked!

Using Date and Time for Benchmarks

```
$start = microtimestamp();
$end = microtimestamp();
($end-$start)
```

Up to now, all date/time functions did not produce results that were more precise than on the second level; no microseconds were available. This changes when you use the function gettimeofday(). This returns an array of values. The key 'sec' returns the associated epoche value; however, 'usec' returns the additional microseconds. With this, a very exact value can be used for operations that need exact measurement, for example, benchmarks.

```php
<?php
  // ...

  $start = microtimestamp();
  $s = '';
  for ($i=0; $i < 100000; $i++) {
   $s .= "$i";
  }
  $end = microtimestamp();
  echo 'Using double quotes: ' . ($end-$start) .
    '<br />';

  $start = microtimestamp();
  $s = '';
  for ($i=0; $i < 100000; $i++) {
   $s .= $i;
  }
  $end - microtimestamp();
  echo 'Using no quotes: ' . ($end-$start) . '<br
    />';
?>
```

Benchmarking Code Using microtimestamp() (benchmark.php; excerpt)

The code at the beginning of this phrase contains a function microtimestamp() that returns an exact time stamp. This function is called twice; in between, a more or less complex calculation is done. The result of this is a benchmark that might help decide which coding technique is superior.

```php
function microtimestamp() {
  $timeofday = gettimeofday();
  return $timeofday['sec'] + $timeofday['usec'] /
    1000000;
}
```

Figure 3.3 shows the result. Your mileage might vary, but you will find that using the double quotes just costs time. (In another experiment, you might also find out that it makes very little difference whether you use single or double quotes—despite popular beliefs.)

Figure 3.3   The second piece of code
is the faster one.

Using Form Fields for
Date Selection

```php
<select name="month"><?php
  for ($i = 1; $i <= 12; $i++) {
    $monthname = date('F', mktime(12, 0, 0, $i, 1,
      2005));
    echo "<option value=\"$i\">$monthname</option>";
    }
?></select>
```

If you want to offer an HTML form to select a date, like many hotel- and flight-booking services offer, you can use the various parameters of date(); loop through all months of the year; and, therefore, create a selection list of days, months, and years. The preceding code contains the code for this; see Figure 3.4 for the result.

```
<form method="post" action="<?php echo
    htmlspecialchars($_SERVER['PHP_SELF']); ?>">
  <select name="day"><?php
    for ($i = 1; $i <= 31; $i++) {
      echo "<option value=\"$i\">$i</option>\n";
    }
  ?></select>
  <select name="month"><?php
    for ($i = 1; $i <= 12; $i++) {
      $monthname = date('F', mktime(12, 0, 0, $i, 1,
        2005));
      echo "<option value=\"$i\">$monthname</
        option>";
    }
  ?></select>
  <select name="year"><?php
    for ($i = 2005; $i <= 2010; $i++) {
      echo "<option value=\"$i\">$i</option>";
    }
  ?></select>
</form>
```

Selecting a Date Using an HTML Form (dateselection.php; excerpt)

> **TIP**
>
> You can replace the `microtimestamp()` function with the following code:
>
> ```
> function microtimestamp() {
>    return microtime(true);
> }
> ```
>
> The function `microtime()` returns a float value of the current microtime, when the parameter `true` is provided (this was added in PHP 5). However, this is reportedly slower than using `gettimeofday()`, which just executes the underlying `gettimeofday` system call.

Create Self-updating Form Fields for Date Selection

The code from the following phrase has one minor flaw: The number of days per month is always from 1 to 31, even in months that have less days. Using JavaScript, it is possible to write a fancy script that calculates how many days the current month has and then updates the selection list.

```php
<?php
  if (isset($_POST['month']) && is_numeric($_POST
  ['month']) &&
    ((int)$_POST['month'] >= 1 &&
(int)$_POST['month'] <= 12)) {
    $month = (int)$_POST['month'];
  } else {
    $month = date('n');
  }
  if (isset($_POST['year']) && is_numeric($_POST
  ['year']) &&
    ((int)$_POST['year'] >= 2005 &&
```

Create Self-updating Form Fields for Date Selection

```php
(int)$_POST['year'] <= 2010)) {
    $year = (int)$_POST['year'];
  } else {
  $year = date('Y');
  }
?>
<form method="post" action="<?php echo
  htmlspecialchars($_SERVER['PHP_SELF']); ?>">
  <select name="day"><?php
    $maxdays = date('t', mktime(12, 0, 0, $month, 1,
      $year));
    for ($i = 1; $i <= $maxdays; $i++) {
      if (isset($_POST['day']) && $_POST['day'] ==
      $i) {
        $sel = ' selected';
      } elseif ($i == date('j')) {
        $sel = ' selected';
      } else {
        $sel = '';
      }
      echo "<option value=\"$i\"$sel>$i</option>\n";
    }
  ?></select>
  // ...
</form>
```

The Date Selection Updates Itself Automatically
(dateselection-js.php; excerpt)

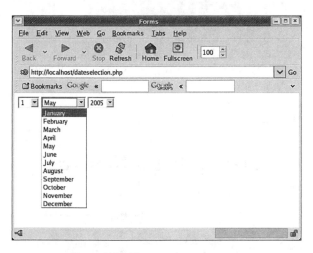

Figure 3.4   The month names were
automatically generated.

However, it is much more convenient to use a combination of JavaScript and PHP. Using JavaScript, you
automatically submit the form. Using PHP, you prefill
the form fields (see Chapter 4, "Interacting with Web
Forms," for more information about that) and, more
importantly, find out how many days the related year
has.

The JavaScript code is limited to a minimum:
Selecting another month submits the HTML form (as
does selecting another year because leap years make
February longer):

```
<select name="month" onchange="this.form.submit();">
...
<select name="year" onchange="this.form.submit();">
```

The number of days per month can be found using date('t'). The listing at the beginning of this phrase contains the complete code for this, including some sanity checks for the information transmitted. Also, the code automatically preselects the current date, unless the user chooses something else. Figure 3.5 contains the output of the complete code.

Calculating the Difference Between Two Dates

```
$century = mktime(12, 0, 0, 1, 1, 2001);
$today = time();
$difference = $today - $century;
```

The epoche value that can be determined by time() and other PHP functions can be used to easily calculate the difference between two dates. The trick is to convert the dates into time stamps (if not already available in this format). Then the difference between these two time stamps is calculated. The result is the time difference in seconds. This value can then be used to find out how many minutes, hours, and days this corresponds to:

- Divide the result by 60 to get the number of minutes
- Divide the result by 60 * 60 = 3600 to get the number of hours
- Divide the result by 60 * 60 * 24 = 86400 to get the number of days

```php
<?php
  $century = mktime(12, 0, 0, 1, 1, 2001);
  $today = time();
  $difference = $today - $century;
  echo 'This century started ';
  echo floor($difference / 84600);
  $difference -= 84600 * floor($difference / 84600);
  echo ' days, ';
  echo floor($difference / 3600);
  $difference -= 3600 * floor($difference / 3600);
  echo ' hours, ';
  echo floor($difference / 60);
  $difference -= 60 * floor($difference / 60);
  echo " minutes, and $difference seconds ago.";
?>
```

The Difference Between Two Dates (timediff.php)

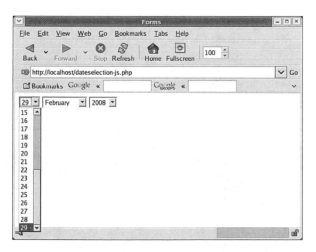

Figure 3.5 The PHP code filled the month selection list with the appropriate number of days.

If you start with the number of days, round down each result and substract this from the result; you can also split up the difference into days, hours, and minutes.

Using GMT Date/ Time Information

Usually, PHP takes the local settings for time formats. However in some special cases, the GMT time format must be used. For this, PHP offers "GMT-enabled" versions of some of its date/time functions:

- gmdate() works like date() and formats a date/time value; however, the return value uses GMT format

- gmmktime() creates a time stamp like mktime(); however, it uses GMT

- gmstrftime() formats a time as strftime() does; however, it uses GMT

GMT is important when it comes to setting a page's expiry date in an HTTP header or manually setting the expiry date of a cookie, also in the HTTP header.

What Does PEAR Offer?

The following PEAR packages offer functionality helpful for processing form data of any kind:

- Date contains a set of functions to work with various date/time values, including conversions between time zones and various date/time representations

- Date_Holidays calculates the names and dates of special holidays

Interacting with Web Forms

HTML forms are one of the key ingredients of any dynamic website because they can enable the users of a site to interact with it. Otherwise, websites are more or less static: They may be driven by a database and, therefore, regularly changing, but they look the same for each and every visitor. HTML forms can change that; therefore, using data from forms from within PHP is very important.

Reading the information in is a very easy task: For form data submitted via GET (that is, in the Uniform Resource Identifer [URI] of the page requested), the data can be found in $_GET[<value of name attribute of form field>]. However, this is only the beginning. Suppose a user fills out a form but forgets one field. Instead of presenting an error message and asking the user to click the browser's Back button, the user can expect a form in which all fields are filled in with the values that he previously provided. Many books neglect this; yet, even worse, some books just do it wrong. You must not forget the special encoding of the form field values; otherwise, the form is subject to Cross-Site Scripting (XSS) attacks or, at least, could look ugly.

Figure 4.1 demonstrates this: You see two buttons with
the same caption; however, only the first button's caption was encoded correctly in the HTML code.

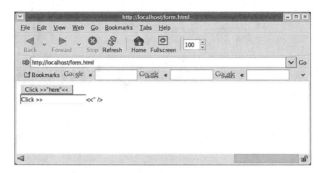

Figure 4.1   Correct encoding of special
characters is mandatory.

Other important topics of interest include Hypertext
Transfer Protocol (HTTP) file uploads and coping
with the various settings in php.ini or elsewhere that
might boycott the good intentions of the developer.

Sending Form Data Back to the Current Script

```
<form action="<?php echo htmlspecialchars($_SERVER
['PHP_SELF']); ?>">
</form>
```

All relevant browsers send back form data to the
current page, if no action attribute is provided in the
<form> element. However, the HTML and the
Extensible Hypertext Markup Language (XHTML)

specifications both state that action is a required attribute (marked as #REQUIRED in the Document Type Definitions [DTDs]). The behavior of the user agent is undefined, as the HTML specification at http://w3.org/TR/html4/interact/forms. html#adef-action explains. Therefore, it's a good idea to specifically provide the uniform resource locator (URL) of the current script as the form's action. the code above does this and also escapes special characters in $_SERVER['PHP_SELF'] for security reasons.

Reading Out Form Data

At the beginning, reading out form data was very easy: If the form field had the name attribute "whatever" or, in newer versions of HTML/XHTML, the id attribute "whatever", PHP creates a variable $whatever in the global scope. This is very convenient, but, from an architectural point of view, is a bad idea. Therefore, this was disabled by default from PHP version 4.2 onward, using the following php.ini directive:

```
register_globals = Off
```

Since PHP 3, the following global arrays existed for form data:

- $HTTP_GET_VARS—All data provided using GET
- $HTTP_POST_VARS—All data provided using POST
- $HTTP_REQUEST_VARS—All data provided using GET or POST, or via cookies (use not recommended)

These arrays are global; therefore, you have to use the global keyword to uplevel them to global scope if you use them within a function:

```
function processData() {
  global $HTTP_POST_VARS;
  // now you may access $HTTP_POST_VARS
}
```

However, these arrays can be deactivated (PHP 5 onward), as well, using this php.ini directive:

```
register_long_arrays = Off
```

Therefore, the following is the only recommended method to access form data today in PHP:

- $_GET for GET data
- $_POST for POST data
- $_REQUEST for POST, GET, and cookies (not recommended)

The keys of these arrays are the names of the form values. The $_* arrays are so-called superglobal arrays—that is, you do not have to use the global keyword to get them into global scope; they are already available within functions.

When you have decided which superglobal array to use (depending on the form's method), accessing form data is easy: $_GET[<formfieldname>] or $_POST[<formfieldname>] retrieves the value in the form element. Table 4.1 shows which data is returned for which form field type.

Table 4.1   Form Field Types and Data Returned in $_GET/$_POST

Form Field Type	Data Returned
Text field	Text in field
Password field	Text in field (clear text, not encrypted)
Multiline text field	Text in field

Table 4.1 Continued

Form Field Type	Data Returned
Hidden field	value attribute of field
Radiobutton	value attribute of selected radio button
Checkbox	value attribute of check box if checked (or "on", if value not set)
Selection list	value attribute of selected list element (or caption of selected list element, if value not set)
Multiple selection list	value attributes of selected list elements as san array (or captions of selected list elements as an array, if values not set)
Submit button	value attribute of Submit button, if this one was used to send the form (important if there is more than one Submit button)

TIP

Two remaining form field types, graphical Submit buttons and file uploads, are covered specifically later in this chapter.

Coping with "Magic Quotes"

```
if (get_magic_quotes_gpc()) {
    $_GET  = stripFormSlashes($_GET);
    $_POST = stripFormSlashes($_POST);
}
```

If the configuration setting magic_quotes is set to "On",
all data coming in from external sources, including

form data and cookies, gets special treatment. All quote characters, " and ', are escaped using the backslash character (\). Therefore, if the user enters It's my life into a text field, the value found in $_GET or $_POST is It\'s my life. This was originally implemented to avoid Structured Query Language (SQL) injection (see Chapter 8, "Using XML," for more details on that), but is—especially for experienced programmers—very annoying. The only thing that is even more annoying is to remove these quotes manually for every form field.

```php
<?php
  function stripFormSlashes($arr) {
    if (!is_array($arr)) {
      return stripslashes($arr);
    } else {
      return array_map('stripFormSlashes', $arr);
    }
  }

  if (get_magic_quotes_gpc()) {
    $_GET  = stripFormSlashes($_GET);
    $_POST = stripFormSlashes($_POST);
  }
?>
```

Stripping Slashes, If They Were Added by "Magic Quotes"
(stripFormSlashes.inc.php)

The PHP function stripslashes() removes escape backslashes from strings. However, this function can only be called if "magic quotes" have been applied; otherwise, it destroys backslashes that were added on purpose. You can determine whether "magic quotes" are active by calling the Boolean function get_magic_quotes_gpc(). If this returns true, all slashes can be removed. To make this as convenient as possible, you can put this in a universal function called stripFormSlashes(). Using array_map(), all elements of an array are unslashed.

This file can then be included into all files that are processing form data and takes care of all "magic quotes" automatically.

Checking Whether a Form Has Been Submitted

```
if (isset($_POST['Submit'])) { …
} else { …
}
```

When both the HTML form and the processing PHP code are on the same page (something that is recommended when it comes to prefilling forms), it is important to find out whether a form is just called in the browser (using GET) or if the form is submitted (and the data must be processed).

```php
<?php
  if (isset($_POST['Submit'])) { …
    echo '<h1>Thank you for filling out this form!
      </h1>';
  } else { …
?>
  <form method="post" action="<?php echo
    htmlspecialchars($_SERVER['PHP_SELF']); ?>">
    <input type="submit" name="Submit" value="Submit
      form" />
  </form>
<?php
  }
?>
```

Checking Whether a Form Has Been Submitted (submit.php; excerpt)

You can take several different approaches to this task; something that always works is assigning the Submit button a name and then testing whether this name is present when the form is submitted.

> **TIP**
>
> If your form has multiple Submit buttons, give each of them a distinctive name; then, you can check specifically for this name and, therefore, determine which Submit button has been used.

Saving Form Data into a Cookie

```
setcookie('formdata', serialize($formdata),
time()+30*24*60*60);
```

After the form has been submitted, the data must go somewhere, possibly in a database (see Chapter 8), in a file, or sent via email. When a website contains several similar forms (for example, forms that all require the user to provide his name and contact information), it is a good idea to save the data after the user fills it in. Because HTTP is a stateless protocol, you have to use cookies (see Chapter 6, "Using Files on the Server File System")—sessions are useless because they expire when the user closes the browser.

```
function setCookieData($arr) {
  $formdata = getCookieData();
  if ($formdata == null) {
    $formdata = array();
  }
```

```
foreach ($arr as $name => $value) {
  $formdata[$name] = $value;
}
setcookie('formdata', serialize($formdata),
  time()+30*24*60*60);
}
```

Saving Data into a Cookie (getFormData.inc.php; excerpt)

Because user agents only have to save 20 cookies per domain, it's a good idea to store the form information in one cookie, in the form of an array. However, only string values are allowed in cookies; this is why you have to serialize the array. The function shown in the listing at the beginning of this phrase writes the contents of the array provided as a parameter into the cookie.

The function getCookieData() returns the existing data from the cookie (if available) and unserializes it into an array. You will see the code in a later phrase.

The only thing left to do is to write the required form data into this array. You can specifically submit only certain values, or the complete array $_GET or $_POST, as shown in the following code.

```
<?php
  require_once 'stripFormSlashes.inc.php';
  require_once 'getFormData.inc.php';
  if (isset($_POST['Submit'])) {
    setCookieData($_POST);
  }
?>
...
<?php
  if (isset($_POST['Submit'])) {
    echo '<h1>Thank you for filling out this
```

```
form!</h1>';
  } else {
?>
  <form method="post" action="<?php echo
    htmlspecialchars($_SERVER['PHP_SELF']); ?>">
  ...
  </form>
<?php
  }
?>
```

Saving Form Data in a Cookie (save-cookie.php; excerpt)

Figure 4.2 shows the resulting cookie.

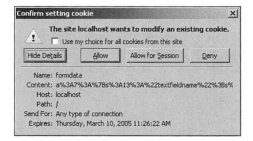

Figure 4.2 The serialized form data
is saved in a cookie.

NOTE

Note that you have to save the form data prior to any
HTML output. As cookies are sent as part of the HTTP
header, they have to be declared before HTML starts (and,
as a matter of consequence, the HTTP header ends). More
information about the timing of cookies can be found in
Chapter 6.

Prefilling Text Fields and Password Fields

```
<input type="text" name="textfieldname"
  value="<?php
  echo (isset($_POST['textfieldname'])) ?
htmlspecialchars($_POST['textfieldname']) : '';
  ?>" />
```

The value in a text field (and in a password field and in a hidden field, as well) is provided in its `value` attribute. However, the data there must be properly encoded with `htmlspecialchars()` to get rid of dangerous characters such as ' or < or >. The code snippet in the preceding code expects the form to be submitted back to itself; thus, it extracts the current value of the text field from `$_POST` (it would work analogously with `$_GET`).

```
<?php
  require_once 'stripFormSlashes.inc.php';
?>
...
<input type="text" name="textfieldname"
  value="<?php
  echo (isset($_POST['textfieldname'])) ?
    htmlspecialchars($_POST['textfieldname']) : '';
  ?>" />
```

Prefilling Text Fields (text.php; excerpt)

TIP

This works for password fields and hidden fields, as well.

If you want to use a default value for this form element, you just have to provide this default value instead of the empty string in the PHP code:

```php
<input type="text" name="textfieldname"
  value="<?php
  echo (isset($_POST['textfieldname'])) ?
    htmlspecialchars($_POST['textfieldname']) :
    'default value';
  ?>" />
```

Another possibility is to prefill form values from cookies. This is quite useful when users enter their data into a form several times. So, when they visit a form on the site a couple of days later, the old data can be retrieved from the cookie. Yes, just one cookie since only 20 cookies per domain are allowed. We use an array for that, of course. However, only strings are allowed as cookie values, so the use of serialize() and unserialize() is required.

The following function retrieves a value from the cookie that contains the form data. The order of precedence is as follows: If $_GET or $_POST contains a current value for this field, this value is used (specific versions of the function exist for $_GET and $_POST because only one of these two methods is normally used at a time). Otherwise, the script looks in $_COOKIE for an associated value. If nothing is found, an empty string is returned.

```php
function getCookieData() {
  if (isset($_COOKIE['formdata'])) {
    $formdata = $_COOKIE['formdata'];
    if ($formdata != '') {
      if (get_magic_quotes_gpc()) {
        $formdata = stripslashes($formdata);
      }
      return unserialize($formdata);
    } else {
      return array();
    }
```

```php
  } else {
    return null;
  }
}

function getFormDataPOST($name) {
  if (isset($_POST[$name])) {
    return $_POST[$name];
  } else {
    $cookiedata = getCookieData();
    if ($cookiedata != null &&
      isset($cookiedata[$name])) {
      return $cookiedata[$name];
    }
  }
  return '';
}
function getFormDataGET($name) {
  if (isset($_GET[$name])) {
    return $_GET[$name];
  } else {
    $cookiedata = getCookieData();
    if ($cookiedata != null &&
      isset($cookiedata[$name])) {
      return $cookiedata[$name];
    }
  }
  return '';
}
```

Retrieving Form Data from a Cookie (getFormData.inc.php; excerpt)

Now, prefilling the form value is easy: Because
getFormDataGET() and getFormDataPOST() always return
anything—including an empty string—the return
value can be directly used in the text field's value
attribute.

```php
<?php
  require_once 'stripFormSlashes.inc.php';
  require_once 'getFormData.inc.php';
?>
...
<input type="text" name="textfieldname"
  value="<?php
    echo
htmlspecialchars(getFormDataPOST('textfieldname'));
  ?>" />
```

Prefilling Text Fields (text-cookie.php; excerpt)

Prefilling Multiline Text Fields

```php
<textarea cols="40" rows="5"
name="areafieldname"><?php
  echo (isset($_POST['areafieldname'])) ?
htmlspecialchars($_POST['areafieldname']) : '';
  ?></textarea>
```

With multiline text fields, almost the same approach as
with single-line text fields and password fields can be
used. The only difference is the location where to put
the prefill value: It belongs between <textarea> and
</textarea>, as shown in the code.

```php
<?php
  require_once 'stripFormSlashes.inc.php';
?>
...
<textarea cols="40" rows="5"
name="areafieldname"><?php
  echo (isset($_POST['areafieldname'])) ?
htmlspecialchars($_POST['areafieldname']) : '';
  ?></textarea>
```

Prefilling Multiline Text Fields (textarea.php; excerpt)

INTERACTING WITH WEB FORMS

> **NOTE**
> If you want to provide a default value in the multiline text field (for example, "Enter your data here …"), provide this instead of the empty string in the PHP code. Remember that line feeds are possible, as well:
>
> ```php
> <?php
>   echo (isset($_POST['areafieldname'])) ?
> htmlspecialchars($_POST['areafieldname']) :
>   "default\nvalue";
> ?>
> ```

Using the combined cookie/GET or cookie/POST approach, the code simplifies a bit.

```php
<?php
  require_once 'stripFormSlashes.inc.php';
  require_once 'getFormData.inc.php';
?>
...
<textarea cols="40" rows="5"
name="areafieldname"><?php
  echo htmlspecialchars(getFormDataPOST
    ('areafieldname'));
  ?></textarea>
```

Prefilling Multiline Text Fields (textarea-cookie.php; excerpt)

Preselecting Radio Buttons

```php
if (isset($_POST['groupname']) &&
    $_POST['groupname'] == 'php5') {
  echo 'checked="checked" ';
}
```

A group of radio buttons is identified by the common name attribute. Out of a group of buttons, only one can

be selected (or none). When submitting a form to the
server, the value attribute of the selected radio buttons
is transmitted to the server. Therefore, it is quite messy
but rather trivial to prefill a group of radio buttons:
Just compare the value in $_GET/$_POST with the associated value. If it fits, print out checked, the HTML
attribute that preselects a radio button, as shown in
the code.

```
<input type="radio" name="groupname" value="php3"
<?php
  if (isset($_POST['groupname']) && $_POST
  ['groupname'] == 'php3') {
    echo 'checked="checked" ';
  }
?>/>PHP 3
<input type="radio" name="groupname" value="php4"
  <?php
  if (isset($_POST['groupname']) &&
$_POST['groupname'] == 'php4') {
    echo 'checked="checked" ';
  }
?>/>PHP 4
<input type="radio" name="groupname" value="php5"
<?php
  if (isset($_POST['groupname']) &&
$_POST['groupname'] == 'php5') {
    echo 'checked="checked" ';
  }
?>/>PHP 5
```

Prefilling Radio Buttons (radio.php; excerpt)

This code can be extended so that a radio button
is preselected when the user has previously saved
his selection in a cookie, using the include file
getFormData.inc.php, as shown in the following code.

```php
<?php
  require_once 'getFormData.inc.php';
?>
...
<input type="radio" name="groupname" value="php3"
  <?php
  if (getFormDataPOST('groupname') == 'php3') {
    echo 'checked="checked" ';
  }
?>/>PHP 3
<input type="radio" name="groupname" value="php4"
  <?php
  if (getFormDataPOST('groupname') == 'php4') {
    echo 'checked="checked" ';
  }
?>/>PHP 4
<input type="radio" name="groupname" value="php5"
<?php
  if (getFormDataPOST('groupname') == 'php5') {
    echo 'checked="checked" ';
  }
?>/>PHP 5
```

Prefilling Radio Buttons (radio-cookie.php; excerpt)

Preselecting Check Boxes

```php
if (isset($_POST['boxname']) && $_POST['boxname']
== 'yes') {
  echo 'checked="checked" ';
}
```

Although some websites pretend to group check boxes like radio buttons, this is technically not true. Every check box stands on its own; therefore, they all should have different names (it would not make sense to give

them identical names). Then each check box can be
treated individually: Check for the associated value
attribute and print out the checked HTML attribute, if
there is a match.

```
<input type="checkbox" name="boxname" value="yes"
  <?php
  if (isset($_POST['boxname']) && $_POST['boxname']
    == 'yes') {
    echo 'checked="checked" ';
  }
?>/>I agree.
```

Prefilling Check Boxes (checkbox.php; excerpt)

When using cookie data (if available), the code
changes slightly.

```
<?php
  require_once 'getFormData.inc.php';
?>
...
<input type="checkbox" name="boxname" value="yes"
  <?php
  if (getFormDataPOST('boxname') == 'yes') {
    echo 'checked="checked" ';
  }
?>/>I agree.
```

Prefilling Check Boxes(checkbox-cookie.php; excerpt)

Preselecting Selection Lists

On a single selection list, the value of the selected
<option> element is transferred to the server when
submitting the form. This value can then be manually

checked to prefill the form, using the `selected` HTML
attribute, as shown in the code.

```
<select name="listname">
  <option value="php3"<?php
  if (isset($_POST['listname'])
    && $_POST['listname'] == 'php3') {
    echo ' selected="selected"';
  }
  ?>>PHP 3</option>
  <option value="php4"<?php
  if (isset($_POST['listname'])
    && $_POST['listname'] == 'php4') {
    echo ' selected="selected"';
  }
  ?>>PHP 4</option>
  <option value="php5"<?php
  if (isset($_POST['listname'])
    && $_POST['listname'] == 'php5') {
    echo ' selected="selected"';
  }
  ?>>PHP 5</option>
</select>
```

Prefilling Selection Lists (select.php; excerpt)

The same effect can be implemented using
`getFormData.inc.php`; then data from the site's cookies
is used, if available.

```
<?php
  require_once 'getFormData.inc.php';
?>
...
<select name="listname">
  <option value="php3"<?php
```

```
  if (getFormDataPOST('listname') == 'php3') {
    echo ' selected="selected"';
  }
  ?>>PHP 3</option>
  <option value="php4"<?php
  if (getFormDataPOST('listname') == 'php4') {
    echo ' selected="selected"';
  }
  ?>>PHP 4</option>
  <option value="php5"<?php
  if (getFormDataPOST('listname') == 'php5') {
    echo ' selected="selected"';
  }
  ?>>PHP 5</option>
</select>
```

Prefilling Selection Lists (select-cookie.php; excerpt)

Preselecting Multiple Selection Lists

```
  if (isset($_POST['multilistname']) &&
in_array('php4', $_POST['multilistname'])) {
    echo ' selected="selected"';
  }
```

When it comes to prefilling form elements, multiple selection lists are the most difficult ones to implement. This is because in $_GET or $_POST, you have an array of chosen options; so you cannot just compare strings, but you have to search for the specified value in the array. Luckily, PHP offers something suitable in the form of the in_array() function. So, the effort required is not much more than with the other form elements: If the current value is in $_GET/$_POST, print out the selected attribute.

```
<select name="multilistname[]" multiple="multiple"
  size="3">
  <option value="php3"><?php
  if (isset($_POST['multilistname']) &&
     in_array('php3', $_POST['multilistname'])) {
    echo ' selected="selected"';
  }
  ?>>PHP 3</option>
  <option value="php4"><?php
  if (isset($_POST['multilistname']) &&
    in_array('php4', $_POST['multilistname'])) {
    echo ' selected="selected"';
  }
  ?>>PHP 4</option>
  <option value="php5"><?php
  if (isset($_POST['multilistname']) &&
    in_array('php5', $_POST['multilistname'])) {
    echo ' selected="selected"';
  }
  ?>>PHP 5</option>
</select>
```

Prefilling Multiple Selection Lists (select-multiple.php; excerpt)

However, the HTML form must be specially prepared to allow PHP to access the data from the multiple selection list: The value of the name attribute has to end with [], hinting to PHP that it should expect an array of values, not just a string value. Accessing the list data, however, can still be done using $_GET['listname']/$_POST['listname'] and not $_GET['listname[]']/$_POST['listname[]'], as shown in the preceding code.

If you want to prefill the list with data from the cookie, you just have to use the well-known file getFormData.inc.php from the previous phrases.

It contains two additional functions that return an array instead of a string.

```php
function getFormDataArrayGET($name) {
  if (isset($_GET[$name])) {
    return $_GET[$name];
  } else {
    $cookiedata = getCookieData();
    if ($cookiedata != null &&
      isset($cookiedata[$name])) {
      return $cookiedata[$name];
    }
  }
  return array();
}
function getFormDataArrayPOST($name) {
  if (isset($_POST[$name])) {
    return $_POST[$name];
  } else {
    $cookiedata = getCookieData();
    if ($cookiedata != null &&
      isset($cookiedata[$name])) {
      return $cookiedata[$name];
    }
  }
  return array();
}
```

Retrieving Form Data from a Cookie (getFormData.inc.php; excerpt)

These functions return an array for multiple lists that you can use as you did in select-multiple.php.

```php
<?php
  require_once 'getFormData.inc.php';
?>
<!DOCTYPE html PUBLIC "-//W3C//DTD XHTML 1.0
```

```
  Transitional//EN" "http://www.w3.org/TR/xhtml1/
  DTD/
xhtml1-transitional.dtd">
<html>
<head>
  <title>Forms</title>
</head>
<body>
  <form method="post" action="
<?php echo htmlspecialchars($_SERVER['PHP_SELF']);
  ?>">
    <select name="multilistname[]"
    multiple="multiple" size="3">
      <option value="php3"<?php
  if (in_array('php3', getFormDataArrayPOST
  ('multilistname'))) {
    echo ' selected="selected"';
  }
    ?>>PHP 3</option>
      <option value="php4"<?php
  if (in_array('php4', getFormDataArrayPOST
  ('multilistname'))) {
    echo ' selected="selected"';
  }
    ?>>PHP 4</option>
      <option value="php5"<?php
  if (in_array('php5', getFormDataArrayPOST
  ('multilistname'))) {
    echo ' selected="selected"';
  }
    ?>>PHP 5</option>
    </select><br />
    <input type="submit" />
  </form>
</body>
</html>
```

Prefilling Multiple Selection Lists (select-multiple-cookie.php; excerpt)

Processing Graphical Submit Buttons

```
if (isset($_POST['Submit_x']) &&
isset($_POST['Submit_y']))
```

Graphical Submit buttons (`<input type="image" />`) are not only a nice way to spicen up the layout of the form, but they also offer a nice feature: The browser submits the x and the y coordinates of the mouse pointer when clicking on the button. In PHP, this happens by appending _x and _y to the `name` attribute of the button and writing this into `$_GET` or `$_POST`. The preceding code evaluates this information.

```php
<?php
  if (isset($_POST['Submit_x']) && isset($_POST
    ['Submit_y'])) {
    printf('<h1>You clicked at the following
      coordinates: x-%s, y-%s</h1>',
      htmlspecialchars($_POST['Submit_x']),
      htmlspecialchars($_POST['Submit_y'])
    );
  } else {
?>
  <form method="post" action="<?php echo
    htmlspecialchars($_SERVER['PHP_SELF']); ?>">
    <input type="image" name="Submit" src="sams.gif"
      />
  </form>
<?php
  }
?>
```

Processing Graphical Submit Buttons (image.php; excerpt)

> **NOTE**
> When you submit the form using the keyboard (for example, with the Enter key), both coordinates are 0.

Checking Mandatory Fields

```
if (isset($_POST['Submit']) &&
    isset($_POST['textfieldname']) &&
    trim($_POST['textfieldname']) != '')
```

When validating a form, most of the time the emphasis is on mandatory fields. You can check if they contain values in two ways:

- Check whether the fields exist in `$_GET`/`$_POST`

```
if (!isset($_GET['fieldname'])) {
  // Error!
}
```

- Check whether the values in `$_GET`/`$_POST` contain information other than whitespace

```
if (trim($_GET['fieldname']) == '') {
  // Error!
}
```

It is very important that you combine **both** techniques. You always have to check for a field's existence using `isset()` to avoid error messages when trying to access array values that do not exist. But you always have to check whether there is something within the field apart from whitespace because text fields are always submitted. In addition, when empty, `isset()` always returns `true` independent of the field's value.

```php
<?php
  if (isset($_POST['Submit']) &&
      isset($_POST['textfieldname']) &&
      trim($_POST['textfieldname']) != '') {
    echo '<h1>Thank you for filling out this
      form!</h1>';
  } else {
?>
  <form method="post" action="
<?php echo htmlspecialchars($_SERVER['PHP_SELF']);
   ?>">
    <input type="text" name="textfieldname"
      value="<?php
  echo (isset($_POST['textfieldname'])) ?
    htmlspecialchars($_POST['textfieldname']) : '';
      ?>" />
    <input type="submit" name="Submit" />
  </form>
<?php
  }
?>
```

Validating Mandatory Fields (mandatory.php; excerpt)

TIP

This methodology also applies for all other text form elements, radio buttons, and check boxes. It can be easily extended to check for certain patterns, including valid email addresses. Refer to Chapter 2, "Working with Arrays," for phrases that can be of assistance here.

NOTE

The code for prefilling the form element has been left intact so that this code snippet can be merged with other code snippets. So, if the form has only partially been filled out, the correct form fields are prefilled.

Checking Selection Lists

```
isset($_POST['listname']) &&
$_POST['listname'] != '')
```

When it comes to validating a selection list, the approach depends on the type of list:

- If it is a list in which only one element may be selected, the list is considered to be filled out incorrectly if
- No option in the list is selected
- The selected option has an empty string as a value
- If it is a list in which multiple elements may be selected, the list is considered to be filled out incorrectly if
- No option in the list is selected
- All selected options have an empty string as a value

Options with empty strings as values come into play if the list contains functionless dummy entries that have captions such as "Please choose from list." These list options must not receive a value other than " ", so that the validation algorithm can distinguish these entries from reasonable ones.

The listing at the beginning of this phrase validates a single selection list—again including PHP code to pre-fill the list.

```php
<?php
  if (isset($_POST['Submit']) &&
      isset($_POST['listname']) &&
      $_POST['listname'] != '') {
    echo '<h1>Thank you for filling out this
```

```
    form!</h1>';
  } else {
?>
  <form method="post" action="<?php echo
    htmlspecialchars($_SERVER['PHP_SELF']); ?>">
    <select name="listname">
      <option value="">Please select from
        list</option>
      <option value="php3"<?php
if (isset($_POST['listname'])
  && $_POST['listname'] == 'php3') {
    echo ' selected="selected"';
}
    ?>>PHP 3</option>
      <option value="php4"<?php
if (isset($_POST['listname'])
  && $_POST['listname'] == 'php4') {
    echo ' selected="selected"';
}
    ?>>PHP 4</option>
      <option value="php5"<?php
if (isset($_POST['listname'])
  && $_POST['listname'] == 'php5') {
    echo ' selected="selected"';
}
    ?>>PHP 5</option>
    </select><br />
    <input type="submit" name="Submit" />
  </form>
<?php
  }
?>
```

Validating Lists (mandatory-list.php; excerpt)

With multiple lists, a bit more work is required, as shown in the following code. If the form has been submitted, the array of selected list elements is searched. If one element that is nonempty is found, the process is complete and the user can be congratulated for the successful completion of the form. Otherwise, the form is displayed again.

```php
<?php
  $ok = false;
  if (isset($_POST['Submit']) &&
      isset($_POST['multilistname'])) {
    if (is_array($_POST['multilistname'])) {
      for ($i=0; $i <
        count($_POST['multilistname']); $i++) {
        if ($_POST['multilistname'][$i] != '') {
          $ok = true;
          break;
        }
      }
    }
  }

  if ($ok) {
    echo '<h1>Thank you for filling out this
      form!</h1>';
  } else {
?>
  <form method="post" action="
<?php echo htmlspecialchars($_SERVER['PHP_SELF']);
  ?>">
    <select name="multilistname[]"
      multiple="multiple" size="5">

    </select>
<br />
    <input type="submit" name="Submit" />
  </form>
<?php
  }
?>
```

Validating Multiple Lists (mandatory-list-multiple.php; excerpt)

Writing All Form Data into a File

```
$data[] = $_POST;
file_put_contents('formdata.txt',
  serialize($data));
```

After a user fills out a form correctly, what do you do with the form data? A very intuitive approach that does not require too much setup on the server is to write the data into a file on the server.

```php
<?php
  require_once 'stripFormSlashes.inc.php';
?>
...
<?php
  if (isset($_POST['Submit']) &&
      isset($_POST['fieldname']) &&
      trim($_POST['fieldname']) != '') {
    echo '<h1>Thank you for filling out this
      form!</h1>';
    $data = '';
    $data = @file_get_contents('formdata.txt');
    if ($data != '') {
      $data = unserialize($data);
    }
    $data[] = $_POST;
    file_put_contents('formdata.txt',
      serialize($data));
  } else {
?>
  <form method="post" action="<?php echo
    htmlspecialchars($_SERVER['PHP_SELF']); ?>">
  ...
  </form>
<?php
  }
?>
```

CHAPTER 4

Writing Form Data into a File (form-save.php; excerpt)

The preceding code contains a very naïve approach: All data is stored in a file on the server. When the form is submitted, the file is read in and unserialized into an array. Then, the form data is appended to the array. Finally, the array is serialized again and written back to the file.

Figure 4.3 shows this file in a text editor.

> **NOTE**
>
> Of course, race conditions could occur and the file could be simultaneously read by two processes, which would result in just one of the two processes appearing in the file. To avoid this, you have to implement file locking as shown in Chapter 7, "Making Data Dynamic."

Figure 4.3 Data written into the form
(can later be unserialized).

Sending All Form Data Via Email

```
mail('recipient@domain.tld', 'Form data', $text);
```

A more imminent notification of someone filling out a form can be implemented by sending form data via email. Of course, you can write a custom mail script for each and every form; however, the preceding code shows how this can be done universally. Via for, all form data is merged into a string. Special care is taken of form values that are arrays—this can occur with multiple selection lists. Then the form data is mailed to the webmaster—just don't forget to change the email address.

CHAPTER 4

```php
<?php
  require_once 'stripFormSlashes.inc.php';
?>
...
<?php
  if (isset($_POST['Submit']) &&
      isset($_POST['fieldname']) &&
      trim($_POST['fieldname']) != '' &&
      $_POST['groupname'] != '') {
    echo '<h1>Thank you for filling out this
      form!</h1>';
    $text = '';
    foreach ($_POST as $name => $value) {
      if (is_array($value)) {
        $text .= sprintf("%s: %s\n", $name, join('
          ', $value));
      } else {
        $text .= sprintf("%s: %s\n", $name, $value);
      }
    }
    mail('recipient@domain.tld', 'Form data',
      $text);
  } else {
?>
  <form method="post" action="<?php echo
    htmlspecialchars($_SERVER['PHP_SELF']); ?>">
  ...
  </form>
```

```
<?php
  }
?>
```

Sending Form Data Via Email (form-mail.php; excerpt)

Getting Information About File Uploads

```
printf('<p>Error: %s<br />
        Original name: %s<br />
        File size: %s<br />
        Temporary name: %s<br />
        MIME type: %s</p>',
  $_FILES['File']['error'],
  $_FILES['File']['name'],
  $_FILES['File']['size'],
  $_FILES['File']['tmp_name'],
  $_FILES['File']['type'])
```

When uploading files to the web server using `<input type="file" />`, the HTML form has to fulfill two requirements:

- The enctype attribute has to be set to "multipart/form-data"

- The method attribute has to be set to "post"

Without these settings, the file upload does not work. It also does not work if the following information is missing from php.ini:

```
file_uploads = On
```

But if it does, retrieving information about the file is quite easy: In the (superglobal) array $_FILES, you can find the file upload form field under its name. Then, the following subkeys provide further information about the uploaded file:

- `$_FILES["File"]["error"]`—Error code (0 in case of success)

- `$_FILES["File"]["name"]`—Original filename

- `$_FILES["File"]["size"]`—Size of the file

- `$_FILES["File"]["tmp_name"]`—Temporary filename where PHP saved the file

- `$_FILES["File"]["type"]`—The file's MIME type as sent by the client, not reliable

```php
<?php
  if (isset($_POST['Submit']) && isset($_FILES
    ['File'])) {
    printf('<p>Error: %s<br />
            Original name: %s<br />
            File size: %s<br />
            Temporary name: %s<br />
            MIME type: %s</p>',
      $_FILES['File']['error'],
      $_FILES['File']['name'],
      $_FILES['File']['size'],
      $_FILES['File']['tmp_name'],
      $_FILES['File']['type']
    );
  } else {
?>
  <form action="<?php echo
    htmlspecialchars($_SERVER['PHP_SELF']); ?>"
    method="post" enctype="multipart/form-data">
    <input type="file" name="File" />
    <input type="submit" name="Submit" value="Submit
      form" />
  </form>
<?php
  }
?>
```

Displaying Information About Uploaded Files (upload.php; excerpt)

The preceding code outputs the available file information (see Figure 4.4).

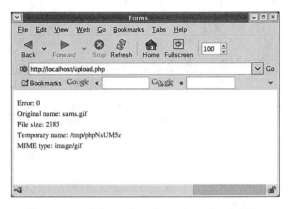

Figure 4.4 Information about the uploaded file.

NOTE

Some caveats apply when working with form fields. There is the possibility to provide a maximum file length for the uploaded files in a hidden form field; however, this check is then executed server-side, so it is definitely better if you do that on your own in your script, using the "type" array subelement.

Also, do not rely on the "name" array subelement because this information (the original filename) can be forged. Even worse, some browsers do not always send the original filename, but the complete path to it. Therefore, always call basename() to extract the filename only.

Moving Uploaded Files to a Safe Location

```
move_uploaded_file(
    $_FILES['File']['tmp_name'],
    '/tmp/' . basename($_FILES['File']['name'])
)
```

When a user uploads a file to a PHP script using the
<input type="file" /> HTML element, PHP stores
the file in a temporary location (set in the php.ini
directive upload_tmp_dir) and deletes it upon completion of script execution. Therefore, you have to access
the uploaded file within the script. To do so, PHP
contains the function move_uploaded_file(), which
moves a file from one location to another. The great
thing about move_uploaded_file() is that the function
first does a sanity check, whether the filename you
provide really is an uploaded file or if a malicious user
just tried to trick you into moving /etc/passwd or
C:\boot.ini somewhere else.

```
<?php
  if (isset($_POST['Submit']) && isset($_FILES
  ['File'])) {
    $move = move_uploaded_file(
      $_FILES['File']['tmp_name'],
      '/tmp/' . basename($_FILES['File']['name'])
    );
    echo '<h1>';
    echo ($move) ? 'Moved' : 'Did not move';
    echo ' the file!</h1>';
  } else {
?>
  <form action="<?php echo htmlspecialchars
    ($_SERVER['PHP_SELF']); ?>"
    method="post" enctype="multipart/form-data">
```

```
    <input type="file" name="File" />
    <input type="submit" name="Submit" value="Submit
      form" />
  </form>
<?php
  }
?>
```

Moving an Uploaded File to a New Location (upload-move.php; excerpt)

Suppose the path /tmp exists and is writable by the web server and the PHP process. Then, the preceding code moves the uploaded file to this directory, using its original filename (and you do not care whether the filename already exists).

What Does PEAR Offer?

The following PEAR packages offer functionality helpful for processing form data of any kind:

- HTML_QuickForm is a very convenient package to create forms using an OOP (object-oriented programming) syntax and includes very mighty validation and processing features

- HTTP_Upload helps to manage file uploads and offers advanced features such as providing valid extensions for uploads

INTERACTING WITH WEB FORMS

127

5

Remembering Users (Cookies and Sessions)

Hypertext Transfer Protocol (HTTP) is a stateless protocol. To say it in a simple way: A client (web browser) connects to a web server, sends a request, and gets a response. Then, the connection is closed. The consequence is the next time the same client sends a request to the same web server, it is a new request, so the web server cannot identify the caller. This is, of course, a problem for applications in which state must be maintained, for instance e-commerce applications with a shopping-cart functionality.

However, you can overcome this limitation in several ways. The basic idea is to send some information with the HTTP response; to try to achieve that, this information is sent back with all subsequent requests to that server. The following possibilities exist:

- Sending the data via POST (that is, a form is required each time)

- Sending the data via GET (that is, by appending this information to the request's uniform resource locator [URL])

- Sending the data as part of the HTTP header (in the form of a cookie)

In real-world projects, one of two methods is used: sessions (via GET or cookies) and cookies.

Understanding Cookies

A cookie is sent as part of the HTTP header and is basically a name-value pair. Their main disadvantage is it is possible to deactivate cookies in the web browser (and also to filter them out in proxy servers). Some people think cookies create privacy issues. Part of this might have been caused by an article written by John Udell in March 1997, in which he wrote that every cookie can be read from every web server, thus there is no privacy. This caused quite a stir, although, unfortunately, the correction two months later did not get that amount of attention.

The fact is that cookies have some limitations:

- Cookies are tied to domains, usually the domain that sent the cookie.

- Cookies can be tied to paths on the web server.

- A cookie contains only text information, 4096 bytes at max (including the cookie name and the = character between the name and value).

- Browsers must only accept up to 20 cookies per domain and 300 cookies in total (although some browsers accept more).

> **NOTE**
>
> The (unofficial) cookie specification goes back to Netscape and is still available at http://wp.netscape.com/newsref/std/cookie_spec.html. There have been attempts to create a special Request for Comment (RFC) for next-generation cookies, but this hasn't found any reasonable browser support yet.

Cookies are sent as part of the HTTP header. If a cookie is set, the HTTP header entry `Set-Cookie` is created. The name and value of the cookie (both strings) follow and, optionally, further information such as expiration date, domain, and path of the cookie. For instance, when visiting http://www.php.net/, the PHP website sends this header entry (your mileage may vary, especially in terms of the language and IP address used):

```
Set-Cookie: COUNTRY=DEU%2C84.154.17.84; expires=Thu,
19-May-05 15:23:29 GMT; path=/; domain=.php.net
```

When the browser (or the user) accepts the cookie, it is then sent back to the server in the HTTP header `Cookie`:

```
Cookie: COUNTRY=DEU%2C84.154.17.84
```

A cookie can have an expiration date. If that is set, the cookie lives up to this date (at most) and is a so-called persistent cookie. After that, the browser automatically deletes the cookie—but this could also happen earlier, for instance when the maximum number of cookies in the browser is reached and the oldest cookies are purged. If, however, no cookie expiration date is set, a so-called session cookie or temporary cookie has been created. This lives as long as the web browser is running. When it is closed, the cookie is deleted.

> **TIP**
>
> To actually see the HTTP headers, you could use special extensions to standard web browsers. For Mozilla browsers (including Firefox), the LiveHTTPHeaders extension available at http://livehttpheaders.mozdev.org/ is a real time-saver. Users of Microsoft Internet Explorer might be interested in installing ieHTTPHeaders, an Explorer bar available from http://www.blunck.info/iehttpheaders.html. Figure 5.1 shows some of the output the Firefox extension shows when accessing the PHP home page.

Figure 5.1 Cookies are set as part of the
HTTP header.

Creating a Cookie

```php
<?php
  setcookie('version', phpversion());
?>
Tried to send cookie.
```

To create a cookie, the PHP function `setcookie()` can be used. It expects the following parameters; however, only the first one is mandatory:

1. The name of the cookie

2. The value of the cookie

3. The expiry date (in UNIX epoche format)

4. The path on the web server from which the cookie may be accessed

5. The domain from which the cookie may be accessed

6. Whether the cookie may only be sent using secure (HTTP Secure [HTTPS]/Secure Sockets Layer [SSL]) connections

The preceding code sets a simple session cookie with the current PHP version as its value.

Figure 5.2 shows a cookie warning in the Firefox browser. You can clearly see the cookie name and script.

Reading Out Cookies

All cookies to which the server has access (not all cookies that are stored in the browser!) are available in the superglobal array `$_COOKIE`. The `foreach` loop reads in all cookies and sends them to the client in an HTML table.

REMEMBERING USERS (COOKIES AND SESSIONS)

```
<table>
<?php
  foreach ($_COOKIE as $name => $value) {
    printf('<tr><td>%s</td><td>%s</td></tr>',
      htmlspecialchars($name),
      htmlspecialchars($value));
  }
?>
</table>
```

Reading Out Cookie (getcookie.php)

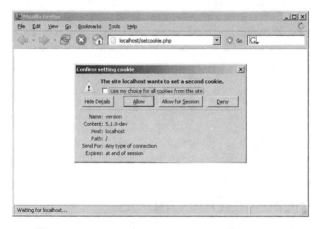

Figure 5.2 Firefox receives the cookie and asks the user what to do.

WARNING

Because cookies are sent as part of the HTTP header, they have to be created before any Hypertext Markup Language (HTML) content is sent out (unless you are using output buffering). Otherwise, you receive an error message such as the one shown in Figure 5.3.

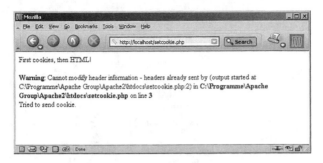

Figure 5.3 Cookies have to be sent prior to any HTML content.

REMEMBERING USERS (COOKIES AND SESSIONS)

NOTE

Usually, PHP takes care of escaping special characters in the cookie values (in URL format). However, since PHP 5, it is possible to do this manually by sending raw cookie data. For this, the function setrawcookie() accepts the same parameter as setcookie(), but does not encode the cookie's value. You must do that manually, with the function urlencode().

Getting Rid of "Magic Quotes" in Cookies

Magic quotes—which were covered and hated in the previous chapter, as well—also apply to cookies because they are data coming from the client. So if magic_quotes is on, single and double quotes are escaped with backslash characters. To get rid of those, this code is used. A similar code was also used in the previous chapter to remove these escape characters from form data (GET and POST data).

If magic_quotes is set, stripslashes() is applied recursively to all data in $_COOKIE.

```php
<?php
  function stripCookieSlashes($arr) {
    if (!is_array($arr)) {
      return stripslashes($arr);
    } else {
      return array_map('stripCookieSlashes', $arr);
    }
  }

  if (get_magic_quotes_gpc()) {
    $_COOKIE  = stripCookieSlashes($_COOKIE);
  }
?>
```

Removing "Magic Quotes" from Cookies (stripCookieSlashes.inc.php)

This file should then be included in all PHP scripts that read cookies, using this statement:

```
require_once 'stripCookieSlashes.inc.php'
```

Setting a (Reasonable) Expiry Date

The expiry date of a cookie is the third parameter for setcookie(). It is an integer value; therefore, the epoche value for a time stamp must be used. Chapter 3, "Date and Time," contains quite a lot of information on how to work with this type of information.

```php
<?php
  setcookie('version', phpversion(), time() +
    21*24*60*60);
?>
Tried to send cookie.
```

Setting a Cookie with a Relative Expiry Date (setcookie-expiry.php)

Usually, it is a good thing to set a relative expiry date for a cookie ("in three weeks") rather than an absolute date ("end of May 2006"). If you use absolute dates, you might have to change your script on a regular basis because the absolute expiry date might arrive soon. It is also considered very unprofessional to set expiry dates that are in the very distant future, for instance in the year 2030. The client that receives this cookie will most certainly not be booted any more in that year.

Therefore, use a relative date. The PHP function time() retrieves the current epoche value; then add to this the number of seconds you want the cookie to live. The code at the beginning of this phrase sets a cookie that will exist for three weeks.

Setting a Client-Specific Expiry Date

```
setcookie('version', phpversion(),
    $_GET['time'] + 21*24*60*60)
```

Keep in mind that the decision of when a cookie expires is made on the client side, using the client time settings. So, if the client has the wrong date (which is something you cannot control from the server-side), your cookies might expire sooner than you expect. So, don't try to set cookies that live for just one hour or so; small things like DST could destroy your plan.

```php
<?php
  if (isset($_GET['time']) && is_int($_GET['time']))
   {
    setcookie('version', phpversion(),
      $_GET['time'] + 21*24*60*60);
  } else {
    setcookie('version', phpversion(),
      time() + 21*24*60*60);
  }
?>
Tried to send cookie.
```

Setting a Cookie with a Specific Expiry Date (setcookie-specific.php)

However, with a bit of JavaScript, it can be possible to avoid this trap. The code in the following listing is client-side JavaScript code that determines the current time (client-side!) as an epoche value and sends it to a server-side script, setcookie-specific.php. The main difference between PHP's time() function and JavaScript's getTime() method is that the latter returns the number of milliseconds since January 1, 1970, whereas the former just works with the number of seconds. So, the JavaScript value first has to be divided by 1,000 and rounded down.

The code for this file can be seen at the beginning of this phrase: The transmitted value is taken as the basis for the calculation of the relative cookie expiration date.

```
<script language="JavaScript"
  type="text/javascript"><!-
  var epoche = (new Date()).getTime();
  epoche = Math.floor(epoche / 1000);
  location.replace("setcookie-specific.php?time=" +
    epoche);
//-></script>
```

Deleting a Cookie

```
setcookie('version', '', time() - 10*365*24*60*60);
```

An intuitive way to delete a cookie is to set its value
to an empty string. However, the cookie is still there,
albeit without a value. A better way is to additionally
send a cookie with the same name again, but provide
an expiry date that is in the past. Again, incorrect local
time settings have to be taken into account, so use a
really small expiry date, for instance 10 years before
today. This listing implements this and deletes the
version cookie that has been sent by the previous
listings. Here, both methods are combined: The cookie
value is set to an empty string, and the expiry date is
in the past. Figure 5.4 shows the result: The browser
tries to delete the cookie by setting the expiry date to
the desired time (which lies in the past, so the cookie
is gone).

```
<?php
  setcookie('version', '', time() -
    10*365*24*60*60);
?>
Tried to delete cookie.
```

Deleting a Cookie (deletecookie.php)

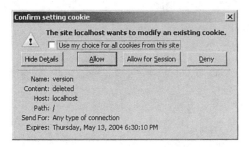

Figure 5.4 The cookie will be deleted (if the user accepts it).

WARNING

If you try to set the expiration date to 0, PHP just skips this parameter, so this does not work. You do have to provide a positive parameter, even if it's 1.

Making Cookies Accessible for Several Domains

```
setcookie('version', phpversion(), 0,
'.example.com');
```

One part of the Set-Cookie header sent by a server is the domain that has access to this cookie. If not sent specifically, this value defaults to the domain that is sending the cookie. Setting this domain to a completely different value, for example, the domain of an ad server (so-called third-party cookies; used to try to generate a profile of the user), does not always work because many browsers allow to specifically disable that. (See Figure 5.5 for an example in the old Netscape 4.x browser that was already capable of doing so.)

```php
<?php
  setcookie('version', phpversion(), 0,
    '.example.com');
?>
Tried to send cookie.
```

Setting the Domain for a Cookie (setcookie-domain.php)

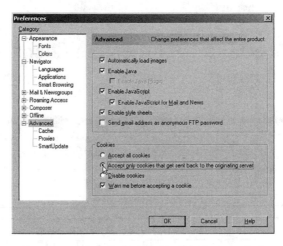

Figure 5.5 Even Netscape 4.x allows you to block
cookies that do not use the originating domain.

REMEMBERING USERS (COOKIES AND SESSIONS)

However, in some instances it is required that the
cookies work on several third-level domains or
subdomains, for instance www.example.com,
store.example.com, and ssl.example.com. Examples for
this are large websites with many subdomains, such as
Amazon and eBay. They require that all top-level
domains (TLDs) are supported. To achieve this,
the domain of the cookie—fourth parameter of
setcookie()—has to be set. Here comes the trick:

All domain names are valid, as long as they contain two dots. So, if you set the domain to ".example.com", all third-level domains of example.com have access to this cookie. There is one "but": Pages on http://example.com/ cannot access this cookie. So, you might want to try to set the domain to "example.com"; however, this does not conform with the specification and might not be supported with all browsers.

Checking Whether the Client Supports Cookies

```
$test_temp = isset($_COOKIE['test_temp']) ?
    'supports' : 'does not support';
$test_persist = isset($_COOKIE['test_persist']) ?
    'supports' : 'does not support';
```

Remember the way cookies are sent: First, the server sends the cookie to the client as part of the HTTP response. In the next request, the client sends the cookie back if accepted. Therefore, calling setcookie() and then checking the contents of $_COOKIE does **not** work. You have to wait for the next HTTP request.

```
<?php
  if (isset($_GET['step']) && $_GET['step'] == '2')
  {
    $test_temp = isset($_COOKIE['test_temp']) ?
      'supports' : 'does not support';
    $test_persist = isset($_COOKIE['test_persist'])
      ?
      'supports' : 'does not support';
    setcookie('test_temp', '', time() -
      365*24*60*60);
    setcookie('test_persist', '', time() -
```

```
   365*24*60*60);
  echo "Browser $test_temp temporary cookies.<br
    />";
  echo "Browser $test_persist persistent
cookies.";
  } else {
    setcookie('test_temp', 'ok');
    setcookie('test_persist', 'ok', time() +
      14*24*60*60);
    header("Location:
      nl2br($_SERVER['PHP_SELF']). "?step=2");
  }
?>
```

Testing the Cookie Configuration of a Browser (cookietest.php)

You can, however, use header() to force the client to
create a second request. In the first request, you set the
cookie; in the second request, you check whether that
worked.

In the previous code, two cookies are set, one temporary cookie and one persistent cookie—because it is
possible to configure some browsers so that one kind
of cookie is accepted, the other one is not. Then, the
redirect is done using header() and the Location:
HTTP header, and the presence of the cookie(s) is
checked.

Of course you should configure your browser to show
a message window when a cookie arrives; that makes
debugging much easier.

Saving Multiple Data in One Cookie

```
setcookie('cookiedata', serialize($cookiedata)
```

Usually, one cookie has one value: one string. Therefore, to store multiple data in cookies, multiple cookies have to be used. This, however, could create some problems, for instance the 20 cookies per domain limit. Therefore, it might make sense to try to save multiple data in one cookie. For this, an array comes to mind.

However, only strings are allowed for the value of a cookie. Therefore, the array must be transformed into a string using serialize() and can then be converted back into an array using unserialize().

CHAPTER 5

```php
<?php
  require_once 'stripCookieSlashes.inc.php';

  function setCookieData($arr) {
    $cookiedata = getAllCookieData();
    if ($cookiedata == null) {
      $cookiedata = array();
    }
    foreach ($arr as $name => $value) {
      $cookiedata[$name] = $value;
    }
    setcookie('cookiedata',
      serialize($cookiedata),
      time() + 30*24*60*60);
  }

  function getAllCookieData() {
    if (isset($_COOKIE['cookiedata'])) {
      $formdata = $_COOKIE['cookiedata'];
```

```
    if ($formdata != '') {
      return unserialize($formdata);
    } else {
      return array();
    }
  } else {
    return null;
  }
}

function getCookieData($name) {
  $cookiedata = getAllCookieData();
  if ($cookiedata != null &&
    isset($cookiedata[$name])) {
      return $cookiedata[$name];
    }
  }
  return '';
}
?>
```

Helper Library to Save Multiple Values into One Cookie (getCookieData.inc.php)

For this, you can write a library that is quite similar to the library used in the previous chapter to save form data in a cookie. One cookie called cookiedata contains all values as an associative array. The function getCookieData() returns one specific value, whereas setCookieData() takes an array and writes its contents to the cookie. The preceding listing shows the complete code for this library.

The following listing uses this library to implement the cookie test from the previous phrase using this library.

```php
<?php
  require_once 'getCookieData.inc.php';

  if (isset($_GET['step']) && $_GET['step'] == '2')
{
    $test = (getCookieData('test') == 'ok') ?
      'supports' : 'does not support';
    echo "Browser $test cookies.";
  } else {
    setCookieData(array('test' => 'ok'));
    header("Location: nl2br($_SERVER['PHP_SELF'].
      "?step=2");
  }
?>
```

Saving the User's Language Preference

```
setcookie('lang', $_SERVER['PHP_SELF'], time() +
30*24*60*60, '/')
```

Many web pages are multilingual. In addition, they are often organized so that every localized section resides in its own directory, similar to this approach:

- The English language version resides in the en directory.

- The Spanish language version resides in the es directory.

- The French language version resides in the fr directory.

You can detect the language of the user in several different ways:

- By trying to tie the client's IP address to a geo-graphical region

- By reading the Accept-Language HTTP header to determine which languages are the preferred ones
- By asking the user

Although all of these methods work somehow, the final one (or a combination of several of them) is considered to be most user-friendly. So, you do need a home page that offers links to all three versions. That's simple HTML, as is shown here:

```
<a href="en/index.php">English version</a><br />
<a href="es/index.php">Versión español</a><br />
<a href="fr/index.php">Versione française</a>
```

Home Page Linking to the Various Language Versions (multilingual.php; excerpt)

Now, every language directory has an index.php file in the specific language. In this file, the code is included from the listing at the beginning of this phrase. This checks whether there is already a language cookie. If not, it tries to set a cookie with the current path (retrieved from $_SERVER['PHP_SELF']).

```php
<?php
  if (!isset($_COOKIE['lang']) ||
    $_COOKIE['lang'] != $_SERVER['PHP_SELF']) {
    setcookie('lang', $_SERVER['PHP_SELF'],
      time() + 30*24*60*60, '/');
  }
?>
```

Saving the Current Path in a Cookie (saveLanguage.inc.php)

REMEMBERING USERS (COOKIES AND SESSIONS)

> **NOTE**
>
> It is important to set the cookie's path to the root directo-
> ry of the web server. Otherwise, the path defaults to the
> current path and the cookie is automatically only readable
> in the current directory and its subdirectories, and not on
> the home page.

Finally, you have to check on the home page to
determine whether the cookie is present, and, if so,
redirect the user to the appropriate page. To do so,
the following code must be added at the top of the
`multilingual.php` page.

```php
<?php
  if (isset($_COOKIE['lang']) && $_COOKIE['lang'] !=
  '') {
    header("Location: ".nl2br($_COOKIE['lang']");
  }
?>
```

Understanding Sessions

Originally, a session is a visit of a user to a website. He
clicks on a few links, has a look at a couple of pages,
and then leaves. This defines a session. Or, to put it in
other words: If a user does not request any data from a
website for a period of time, for example 20 minutes,
the session ends.

HTTP does not know any kind of session mechanism;
the protocol is stateless. However, PHP comes with a
built-in session support that makes it fairly easy to use
sessions.

After a session is created, PHP generates a session ID,
that is, a long string that identifies the session. PHP

then creates a file or a database entry for this session. Then, the PHP application can store data in this session. This data is then written either into the session file or into the database (shared memory is another, but rarely used option).

So, the only thing that must be transported between the client and the server is the session ID. All other data relevant to the session resides at the server. So, no sensitive data is sent over the wire an unnecessary amount of times.

The configuration of PHP's session mechanism is completely triggered in the [session] section of the php.ini configuration file. The default settings might not be suitable for all applications, so the next few phrases cover some possible configurations.

Where to Store the Sessions

Usually, session data is stored in files. The location of these files is set in the php.ini directive session.save_path. Of course, this path must *(a)* exist and *(b)* be readable and writable for the PHP process (usually, the process of the web server). Otherwise, the session information cannot be stored.

However, when you have a lot of users and, therefore, a lot of sessions, PHP should not put all session files in one directory because this might cause some serious performance issues. The following syntax allows PHP to move session data into many subdirectories:

```
session.save_path = "n;/tmp"
```

This creates subdirectories up to the level of n within the /tmp directory. However, these subdirectories have to exist so that PHP's session mechanism can write into them; for this, there exists the shell script mod_files.sh in the ext/session directory.

Of course, only the web server should be allowed to read this directory; otherwise, other users in the system could be able to read session information with possibly sensitive data.

How to Maintain the Session State

The session ID has to be sent to the browser with every response and—much more importantly—has to be sent back to the server with every request.

The easiest way to do so is to use cookies. PHP then sends a cookie with the name PHPSESSID (can be changed with the directive session.name) to the client. However, for this to happen, the following php.ini directive must be set:

```
session.use_cookies = 1
```

However, what happens if the client does not support cookies? Then, a second mechanism comes into play, in the form of the following directive:

```
session.use_trans_sid = 0
```

Then, PHP automatically falls back into a mode in which the session ID is appended automatically to all URLs. This could create some potential security risks (session fixation and session hijacking, for example), but is also quite practical. All relevant e-commerce websites use this mechanism, for instance Amazon. If you go to their website and load a page, the session ID is automatically appended to the end of the URL.

To be able to use session.user_trans_sid, PHP must be compiled with the switch –enable-trans-sid, something that is automatically done for the Windows and Mac OS X binaries.

The other option is to allow only cookies, not session IDs, in URLs. To do so, you can use the following php.ini directive:

```
session.use_only_cookies = 1
```

> **NOTE**
>
> Session IDs in the URL are generally a bad thing; because people could bookmark this information, some search engines will not include your sites, and so on. However, every e-commerce website (and most other websites as well) must take into account that some visitors (potential clients!) just do not like or do not support cookies. Here, sessions offer a convenient way to overcome this limitation.

Activating Sessions

```
session_start()
```

Using session management always requires resources and, therefore, costs performance. Therefore, sessions have to be activated. Because cookies might be part of the package, this has to be done before any HTML content is sent to the client. This can be accomplished in two ways:

- Activate sessions globally with the php.ini directive session.auto_start = 1.

- Activate sessions on a per-script basis with the function `session_start()`.

From a performance point-of-view, the latter option is the best one.

```php
<?php
  session_start();
  echo 'Sessions activated.';
?>
```

Activating Sessions (session_start.php)

Reading and Writing Sessions

```php
<?php
  session_start();
  echo 'Sessions activated.<br />';
  $_SESSION['version'] = phpversion();
  echo 'Session data written.<br />';
  echo "Session data read: {$_SESSION['version']}.";
?>
```

All session data is accessible from a PHP script via the `$_SESSION` array. Because the data itself is stored on the server-side, you can write session data and read it in the next PHP statement, without the requirement of a round-trip to the server as it was with cookies. Just remember to call `session_start()` first and then access `$_SESSION`. The preceding listing creates a session file that Figure 5.6 shows.

Figure 5.6 The content of the session
file created by Listing 5.16.

Closing Sessions

session_destroy()

In some instances, for example when a user logs out,
all session data should be removed, and the session
must be closed. Of course, it would be possible to loop
through $_SESSION with foreach and then set each
value to an empty string or null, but there is a quicker
way: Call session_destroy(). After that, all data in
the current session is destroyed, as the function name
suggests.

```php
<?php
  session_start();
  echo 'Before: <pre>';
  print_r($_SESSION);
  echo '</pre>After: <pre> ';
  session_destroy();
  print_r($_SESSION);
  echo '</pre>';
?>
```

Removing All Session Data (session_destroy.php)

Changing the Session ID

session_regenerate_id()

One common attack against websites that are secured with sessions is that the session ID of a user is somehow taken (for instance, by analyzing HTTP_REFERER entries in HTTP requests) and then used to impersonate that specific user. This is hard to battle, but one convenient way to make it harder for attackers is to change the session ID whenever something "important" happens, such as the user signing in. For instance, Amazon requires users who are already authenticated with their cookie to sign in again when they want to order something.

```php
<?php
  ob_start();
  session_start();
  echo 'Old: ' . session_id();
  session_regenerate_id();
  echo '<br />New: ' . session_id();
  ob_end_flush();
?>
```

Changing the Session ID (session_regenerate_id.php)

In this case, the function session_regenerate_id() just changes the current session ID but leaves all data intact. This is shown in the preceding code, in which the current session ID (both old and new) is retrieved using the session_id() function. Figure 5.7 shows a possible output of this script.

NOTE

This code uses output buffering—ob_start() and ob_end_flush()—because session_regenerate_id() must also be called before any HTML output is sent to the client.

Figure 5.7 Two session IDs, one is old and one is new.

Creating Dynamic, Session-Aware Links

```
$name = urlencode(session_name());
$id = urlencode(session_id());
echo "<a href=\"page.php?$name=$id\">dynamic
  link</a>";
```

Using session.use_trans_sid to automatically update all links to contain the session ID, if required, is a good thing; however, it does not work if those links are dynamically generated by PHP. However, PHP offers two functions that provide all information that is needed:

- session_name() returns the name of the session.
- session_id() returns the current session's ID.

Therefore, the preceding code creates a dynamic link that contains this information, enabling the programmer to make dynamic links session-aware.

One potential output of this code is the following:

```
<a href="page.php?PHPSESSID=
   5b25b64843fad0d1afb4286cfe0ed448">dynamic
   link</a>
```

> ### TIP
>
> When you use an HTML form, PHP automatically appends the session ID to the action attribute of the form. However, if you want to use dynamic forms, you can add a hidden form field to the form, containing the session information:
>
> ```
> <?php
>   $name = htmlspecialchars(session_name());
>   $id = htmlspecialchars(session_id());
>   echo "<input type=\"hidden\" name=\"$name\"
>     value=\"$id\" />";
> ?>
> ```

Implementing a Custom Session Management

```
session_set_save_handler(
  'sess_open', 'sess_close', 'sess_read',
  'sess_write', 'sess_destroy', 'sess_gc');
```

There are some good reasons not to store session data in files. Performance might be one issue, with security as another issue. An alternative way to store session information is to use databases. For this, you just need a database table called sessiondata with three columns (the names might vary, but they have to be used in the upcoming listings):

- Column id (primary key) is of type VARCHAR(32) and contains the session ID.

- Column data is of type TEXT and contains the session data.

- Column access is of type VARCHAR(14) and contains the time stamp of the most recent access to the session information.

It doesn't matter which database is used. This phrase uses MySQL and PHP5's new mysqli extension; however, it is trivial to change the code to work with other databases, as well (see Chapter 7, "Making Data Dynamic," for information about using many relevant databases with PHP).

The PHP function `session_set_save_handler()` can be used to provide custom functions for all relevant six session operations PHP uses internally:

- Opening a session
- Closing a session
- Reading a session variable
- Writing a session variable
- Destroying a session
- Cleaning up (garbage collection, for example removing old session data from the data store)

For all these six operations, the following listing contains code that reads and writes session data from and to a MySQL data source. You just need PHP 5 and have to set the connection parameters (server, username, password) appropriately. Then, you include the code from this listing using `require_once` and then use sessions as usual. In the background, PHP then saves all session information in the database and not in the file system.

```php
<?php
  $GLOBALS['sess_server'] = 'localhost';
  $GLOBALS['sess_db'] = 'sessions';
  $GLOBALS['sess_username'] = 'user';
  $GLOBALS['sess_password'] = 'pass';

  function sess_open() {
    $GLOBALS['sess_mysqli'] = mysqli_connect(
      $GLOBALS['sess_server'],
      $GLOBALS['sess_username'],
      $GLOBALS['sess_password']
    );
```

```php
    mysqli_select_db($GLOBALS['sess_mysqli'],
$GLOBALS['sess_db']);
  }

  function sess_close() {
    mysqli_close($GLOBALS['sess_mysqli']);
  }

  function sess_read($id) {
    $result = mysqli_query(
      $GLOBALS['sess_mysqli'],
      sprintf('SELECT data FROM sessiondata WHERE
        id = \'%s\'',

mysqli_real_escape_string($GLOBALS['sess_mysqli'],
  $id))
    );
    if ($row = mysqli_fetch_object($result)) {
      $ret = $row->data;
      mysqli_query(
        $GLOBALS['sess_mysqli'],
        sprintf('UPDATE sessiondata SET access=\
          '%s\' WHERE id=\'%s\'',
          date('YmdHis'),

mysqli_real_escape_string($GLOBALS['sess_mysqli'],
  $id))
      );
    } else {
      $ret = '';
    }
    return $ret;
  }
```

```php
function sess_write($id, $data) {
  mysqli_query(
    $GLOBALS['sess_mysqli'],
    sprintf('UPDATE sessiondata SET data=\'%s\',
      access=\'%s\' WHERE id=\'%s\'',
mysqli_real_escape_string($GLOBALS['sess_mysqli'],
  $data),
      date('YmdHis'),
mysqli_real_escape_string($GLOBALS['sess_mysqli'],
  $id))
  );
  if (mysqli_affected_rows($GLOBALS
        ['sess_mysqli']) < 1) {
    mysqli_query(
      $GLOBALS['sess_mysqli'],
      sprintf('INSERT INTO sessiondata (data,
        access, id) VALUES (\'%s\', \'%s\',
        \'%s\')',
mysqli_real_escape_string($GLOBALS['sess_mysqli'],
  $data),
      date('YmdHis'),
mysqli_real_escape_string($GLOBALS['sess_mysqli'],
  $id))
    );
  }
  return true;
}
function sess_destroy($id) {
  mysqli_query(
    $GLOBALS['sess_mysqli'],
    sprintf('DELETE FROM sessiondata WHERE
      id=\'%s\'',
mysqli_real_escape_string($GLOBALS['sess_mysqli'],
  $id))
  );
  return true;
}
```

```
function sess_gc($timeout) {
  $timestamp = date('YmdHis', time() - $timeout);
  mysqli_query(
    $GLOBALS['sess_mysqli'],
    sprintf('DELETE FROM sessiondata WHERE access
      < \'%s\'',
      $timestamp)
  );
}

session_set_save_handler(
  'sess_open', 'sess_close', 'sess_read',
  'sess_write', 'sess_destroy', 'sess_gc');
?>
```

TIP

The file session.sql in the download archive contains an
SQL file to create the database table in MySQL. The file
session_mysqli_readwrite.php uses the code in the
preceding listing and saves some data in the session.

Figure 5.8 shows the contents in the session table after
data has been written into it.

Figure 5.8   The session data now
resides in the database.

Creating a Secured Area with Sessions

```
session_start();
if (!(isset($_SESSION['authorized']) &&
  $_SESSION['authorized'] != '')) {
  header("Location:
login.php?url=".nl2br($_SERVER['PHP_SELF']);
}
```

Sessions can be a great way to secure certain parts of a
website. The approach is simple: After the user is
authenticated, write this information into a session
variable. On all protected pages, check for the presence
of this session variable.

First, you can check for the session variable. The code from the beginning of this phrase must be included (with require_once) in all pages that are only accessible for authorized users.

The script login.php, to which the preceding code redirects the user, contains an HTML form (see also Figure 5.9) and checks whether the provided data is correct (you might have to add your own users and passwords). As you might have seen, the previous URL is provided as a GET parameter, so, if available, the login code redirects the user back to where she came from:

```php
<?php
  if (isset($_POST['user']) && $_POST['user'] ==
    'Damon' &&
      isset($_POST['pass']) && $_POST['pass'] ==
        'secret') {
    session_start();
    $_SESSION['authorized'] = 'ok';
    $url = (isset($_GET['url'])) ?
      $nl2br($_GET['url']) :
      'index.php';
    header("Location: $url");
  }
?>
```

Checking the User Credentials (login.php; excerpt)

And that's it! The script secret.php in the download archive contains some quite secret information and is protected by the code in the previous listings.

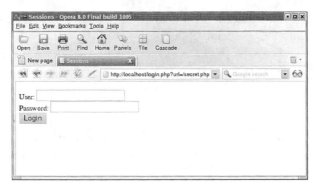

Figure 5.9   The login form—note the referring page
in the URL.

Creating a Secured Area Without Sessions

```
$_SERVER['PHP_AUTH_USER'] == 'Shelley' &&
    $_SERVER['PHP_AUTH_PW'] == 'TopSecret'
```

If using authentication with PHP's session management seems to be too much overhead, you have two other options. First, configure your web server so that only authorized users can access some files or directories. For instance, Apache users might use .htaccess files; http://apache-server.com/tutorials/ATusing-htaccess.html contains some good information about that. Microsoft IIS offers a graphical user interface (GUI) administration of access rights, so that can be done, as well.

```php
<?php
if (!(isset($_SERVER['PHP_AUTH_USER']) &&
    isset($_SERVER['PHP_AUTH_PW']) &&
    $_SERVER['PHP_AUTH_USER'] == 'Shelley' &&
    $_SERVER['PHP_AUTH_PW'] == 'TopSecret')) {
  header('WWW-Authenticate: Basic realm="Secured
    area"');
  header('Status: 401 Unauthorized');
} else {
?>
<!DOCTYPE html PUBLIC "-//W3C//DTD XHTML 1.0
Transitional//EN" "http://www.w3.org/TR/
xhtml1/DTD/xhtml1-transitional.dtd">
...
<?php
}
?>
```

Using HTTP to Secure PHP Pages (http_authentication.php; excerpt)

However, one more or less platform-independent
way is to use authentication via HTTP. If you
send an HTTP status code 401 (unauthorized),
browsers prompt the client for a username and
a password. This information is then available
using $_SERVER['PHP_AUTH_USER'] and
$_SERVER['PHP_AUTH_PW']—however, only if you
are running PHP as a server module, not in
Common Gateway Interface (CGI) mode.

You can then check this and decide whether to send out a 401 header again or to show the page's actual contents. The preceding listing shows an implementation for that. Figure 5.10 shows the prompt for username and password.

Figure 5.10   The browser prompts for a username and a password.

What Does PEAR Offer?

The following PEAR packages offer functionality that can be associated to sessions and HTTP authentication:

- Auth implements various ways to authenticate users and, therefore, protect PHP pages.
- HTTP_Session is based upon PHP's session mechanism but offers an object-oriented access to session information.

REMEMBERING USERS (COOKIES AND SESSIONS)

167

Using Files on the Server File System

Although databases are very common, using the file system to store data can be a real alternative. Often, it is easier to implement that way. Sometimes, it is faster, and much more importantly, all hosting providers have file access enabled, whereas database support might only be available at extra cost.

PHP supports working with files through a set of certain functions. Using wrappers, the same technologies can also be used to access remote data via protocols like Hypertext Transfer Protocol (HTTP) or File Transfer Protocol (FTP), but this is covered in more detail in Chapter 9, "Communicating with Others."

This chapter covers both standard tasks such as reading and writing files, and advanced tasks such as archiving files in ZIP or BZ2 format. Many of these tasks can be solved in different, equally usable ways, so you truly have the freedom of choice.

Opening and Closing Files

```
($fp = @fopen('file.txt', 'at')
fclose($fp);
```

For most file system functions, the files have to be opened first. The function fopen() does exactly this and returns a so-called file handle, a pointer to the file. This file handle can then be used in subsequent functions to, for instance, read information from a file or write to it.

fopen() expects at least two parameters:

- The name of the file
- The file mode to use when accessing the file

```php
<?php
  if ($fp = @fopen('file.txt', 'at')) {
    echo 'File opened.';
    fclose($fp);
    echo '<br />File closed.';
  } else {
    echo 'Error opening file.';
  }
?>
```

Opening (and Closing) Files (fopen.php)

Of great interest is the file mode parameter. This is a string that consists of one or more characters. The first character is one of a, r, w, or x; after that, one or more special modifiers can be used. Table 6.1 shows all modes.

CHAPTER 6

Table 6.1   File Modes for PHP's File Functions

Mode	Description
a	Open file to append (write) data; create it if it doesn't exist
a+	As mode a, but additionally with read access to the file
r	Open file to read data
r+	As mode r, but in addition with write access to the file
w	Open file to write data, erasing its contents; create it if it doesn't exist
w+	As mode w, but in addition with read access to the file
x	Create file to write data; send E_WARNING if it already exists
x+	As mode x, but in addition with read access to the file

So the modifier + always adds the missing read or write access to a file mode. There are other modifiers, as well. As of PHP 4.3.2, PHP does a really good job determining whether a file is a text file or a binary file and translates funny characters appropriately. If you append b to a file mode, you force PHP to open a file as a binary file; for instance, the file mode rb opens a file for reading in binary mode.

Another special modifier exists that might come in handy for Windows users: t. If this is appended to the file mode, all \n line breaks are converted into \r\n as Windows applications might expect.

fopen() returns a file handle or false if opening the file did not work. You should, however, suppress any potential error messages with the @ character, or, in PHP 5, use a try-catch block.

As soon as a file is not used anymore, it should be closed. PHP automatically closes all open files upon termination of the script; however, to use the system resources as efficiently as possible, files should be closed as early as possible to free up memory and speed up the system. For this, use fclose() and provide the file handle as a parameter.

The code at the beginning of this phrase uses both fopen() and fclose().

After running the script, a file called file.txt is created.

> **NOTE**
>
> For this (and other examples in this chapter) to work, you have to make sure that the PHP script has the appropriate rights for the file to access. Usually, Apache runs either under the special user id 0 (UNIX/Linux) or under a regular user account (Windows). Use chmod to set the access privileges accordingly.
>
> Microsoft IIS (Internet Information Services) runs PHP scripts under a special guest account called IUSR_<name of machine>. You can use the graphical user interface shown in Figure 6.1 to tune the access settings for files or directories.

TIP

To avoid any mistakes when trying to access nonexisting files, you can use the function file_exists(), which returns regardless of whether a given filename exists.

```
if (file_exists('file.txt'), 'r') {
   // ...
}
```

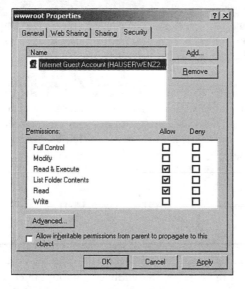

Figure 6.1   Allowing the IIS user to access a file or directory.

Reading from Files

```
echo file_get_contents('file.txt');
```

To read data from a file, PHP offers several possibilities. Probably the easiest way is to read it all at once and then output it to the user.

The function file_get_contents(), available since PHP 4.3.0, returns the contents of a file (or stream) as a string so that it all can be processed further. The preceding code reads in a file called file.txt and prints out its contents. This function is binary-safe, that's why no file mode can (or has to) be used.

The file() function works as file_get_contents(), but returns the file's contents as an array: Each element is one row in the file (including the line break character). The following code converts this array into a string and sends it to the browser. The function implode() glues the array element together (see Chapter 2, "Working with Arrays").

```php
<?php
  echo implode('', file('file.txt'));
?>
```

An even shorter way is to use readfile(), which sends the file's contents directly to the browser. To be able to process the data before sending it, output buffering must be used. The following listing converts special Hypertext Markup Language (HTML) characters and uses <br> elements at line breaks so that the original content of the file is shown in the browser.

```php
<?php
  ob_start();
  readfile('text.txt');
  $data = ob_get_contents();
  ob_end_flush();
  echo nl2br(htmlspecialchars($data));
?>
```

Sending a File's Contents to the Browser Using Output Buffering (readfile.php)

For maximum flexibility, the manual way can be used; however, for text files, this is often not needed. Open the file with fopen(), then call fgets() as long as data is returned (a while loop is convenient here) and output the data. fgets() returns as many characters as are provided in its second parameter but, at most, all characters until the end of the current line.

```php
<?php
  $fp = fopen('file.txt', 'r');
  while (!feof($fp)) {
    $line = fgets($handle, 4096);
    echo $line;
  }
  fclose($fp);
?>
```

Sending a File's Contents to the Browser, Line-by-Line (readfile-linebyline.php)

Writing to Files

```php
file_put_contents('file.txt',
    "-> This text file contains\nsome random text.
<-");
```

Writing to files is as easy as reading from them—if you are using PHP 5 or higher. Then, the function file_put_contents() writes data directly to a file, and this is binary-safe. After calling the function, the file is closed. The code writes data into a file.

```php
<?php
  file_put_contents('file.txt',
    "-> This text file contains\nsome random text.
      <-");
  echo 'File written.';
?>
```

Writing Data into a File (file_put_contents.php)

However, the preceding code overwrites the existing file. If you want to append data (therefore emulating file mode a), you first have to read in the file's data.

```php
<?php
  function file_append_contents($filename, $data) {
    $olddata = @file_get_contents($filename);
    return file_put_contents($filename,
      "$olddata$data");
  }

  file_append_contents('file.txt',
    "\n-> This text file contains\neven more random
      text. <-");
  echo 'Data appended to file';
?>
```

Appending Data to a File (file_append_contents.php)

TIP

It is even easier to provide a third parameter to
file_put_contents() to append data instead of
overwriting files:

```
file_put_contents($filename, $data, FILE_
    APPEND);
```

However, this all fails when a PHP version below 5.0.0
is used because the function file_put_contents() does
not exist in earlier versions. It is, however, possible to
emulate the behavior of file_put_contents() for older
PHP versions. This works similarly to reading from a
file with fopen(), fgets(), and fclose(). For writing,
just one more function is required: fwrite() writes
data to a file handle. The following code implements
this approach. Using function_exists(), can check
whether the function file_put_contents() already
exists. If not, you can write it.

```php
<?php
  if (!function_exists('file_put_contents')) {
    function file_put_contents($filename, $content)
      {
      if ($fp = @fopen($filename, 'w')) {
        $result = fwrite($fp, $content);
        fclose($fp);
        return $result;
      } else {
        return false;
      }
    }
  }
```

```
  file_put_contents('file.txt',
    "\n-> This text file contains\nsome random text.
      <-");
  echo 'Data written to file.';
?>
```

*Using file_put_contents() with All Relevant PHP Versions
(file_put_contents_compatible.php)*

Locking Files

```
flock($fp, LOCK_UN);
```

While reading and writing files, you have to take concurrency into mind. What if two processes try to access the file at the same time? To avoid trouble when one process writes while the other one reads, you have to lock the file. This is done using the PHP function flock().

```php
<?php
  if (!function_exists('file_put_contents')) {
    function file_put_contents($filename, $content)
      {
      if ($fp = @fopen($filename, 'w') && flock($fp,
        LOCK_EX)) {
        $result = fwrite($fp, $content);
        flock($fp, LOCK_UN);
        fclose($fp);
        return $result;
      } else {
        return false;
      }
    }
  }
?>
```

Using file_put_contents() with a File Lock (flock.php; excerpt)

The first parameter is the file handle; the second one is the desired kind of locking to be used. The following options are available:

- LOCK_EX—Exclusive lock for writing
- LOCK_NB—Nonblocking lock
- LOCK_SH—Shared lock for reading
- LOCK_UN—Releasing a lock

The preceding code contains an updated version of the custom file_put_contents() function from the previous phrase, this time using an exclusive lock.

Using Relative Paths for File Access

```
dirname(__FILE__);
basename(__FILE__);
```

Usually, files are opened (or searched) relative to the path of the document. If you are using PHP as an ISAPI module under Windows, the location of php4ts.dll or php5ts.dll may be relevant. To be sure that you are searching to the current scripts' path, you can use a two-step approach:

- The constant __FILE__ contains the full path of the current script
- The function dirname() determines the directory name portion of a path

```php
<?php
  $directory = dirname(__FILE__);
  $filename = basename(__FILE__);
  print "This script is called $filename and resides
    in $directory.";
?>
```

Determining Directory Name and Filename (pathinfos.php)

To use a relative path, you can now call dirname(__FILE__) and then attach the relative path, taking into consideration the directory separator character, which is / on UNIX/Linux, \ on Windows, and : on Mac OS X. Usually, / works fine on most systems, but you should note the requirements of the system on which you want to host your site.

The sister function to dirname() is basename(); this one determines the filename portion of a path.

The listing at the beginning of this phrase uses both basename() and dirname() and __FILE__ to determine information about the current path: directory and filename. Figure 6.2 shows the script's output.

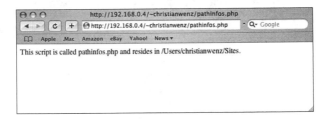

Figure 6.2 Detecting the script's name and its directory.

CHAPTER 6

Avoiding Security Traps with File Access

One very important point: If you are using files with PHP, avoid retrieving the filename from external sources, such as user input or cookies. This might allow users to inject dangerous code in your website or force you to load files you did not want to open. Some so-called security experts had a self-programmed content management system that created uniform resource locators (URLs) like this: index.php?page=subpage.html. This just loaded the page subpage.html into some kind of page template and sent this to the browser. But what if the following URL is called: index.php?page=../../../etc/passwd? With some luck (or bad luck, depending on your point of view), the contents of the file /etc/passwd are printed out in the browser. This kind of attack—a so-called directory traversal attack—is quite common on the Web. However, you can avoid becoming a victim in several ways:

- If possible, do not use dynamic data in filenames.

- If you have to use dynamic data in filenames, use basename() to determine the actual name of the file, omitting the path information.

- Set the php.ini directive open_basedir. This expects a list of directories where PHP may access files. PHP checks the basedir rules whenever a file is opened, and refuses to do so if it isn't in the appropriate path.

- Set include_path to a directory you put all to-be-used files into and set the third parameter to fopen() to true, using the include_path.

Working with CSV Data

```
fgetcsv($handle, 4096);
```

CSV is a file format and stands for comma separated values. Many spreadsheet applications can export their data into CSV files. It seems to be easy to use explode() to convert CSV values into arrays; however, this turns out to be really complicated. What if there is a comma within a value? Then, the content is surrounded by double quotes, which makes it hard to use explode().

```
<table>
<?php
  $fp = fopen('file.csv', 'r');
  while (!feof($fp)) {
    $line = fgetcsv($handle, 4096);
    echo '<tr><td>';
    echo implode('</td><td>', htmlspecialchars
      ($line));
    echo '</td></tr>';
  }
  fclose($fp);
?>
</table>
```

Reading CSV Information (fgetcsv.php)

As (almost) always, the PHP project has done most of the work and offers fgetcsv(). This function works as fgets(); however, it converts the line into an array, separating the contents at a comma (or any other character provided in the third parameter).

The second parameter to fgetcsv() is the maximum length of a line in the CSV file. This is optional in PHP 5.0.0 and later, but before, that had to be set. So you need to check the length of the longest line in the CSV file; otherwise, data will get truncated.

The code at the beginning of this phrase reads in a CSV file and outputs it as an HTML table. This is done using the following code within a loop:

```
$line = fgetcsv($handle, 4096);
echo '<tr><td>';
echo implode('</td><td>', $line);
echo '</td></tr>';
```

This creates a row in an HTML table:
`<tr><td>...</td></tr>`.

Figure 6.3 shows both the original spreadsheet file (in OpenOffice.org) and the result in the browser.

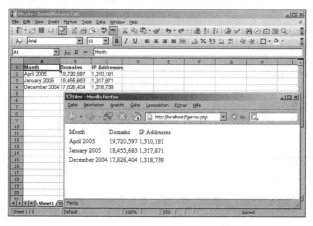

Figure 6.3 The CSV spreadsheet in OpenOffice.org and the result in the browser (`fgetcsv.php`; excerpt).

> **NOTE**
>
> In the code at the beginning of this phrase, the output is
> not sanitized using `htmlspecialchars()`—in this case, to
> make the code short. However, depending on the data you
> have, you should consider running `htmlspecialchars()`
> on all elements of the array's `fgetcsv()` returns.

For writing PHP files, PHP offers a sister function,
`fputcsv()`. You provide a file pointer and an array of
values, and PHP does the rest, including escaping
special characters. Unfortunately, this function currently only resides in PHP's CVS, so at the time of this
writing, you have to manually emulate this behavior.
Basically, you just join all array elements with commas.
You also have to take care of commas within the elements, so you surround all values by double quotes. If
the element contains double quotes, these have to be
escaped. However, this is not done using backslashes,
but by doubling the quotes. The following is an example for a valid line of CSV data:

```
Quote,"And she said: ""No."" ...",Unknown
```
The following is the code for `fputcsv()`:

```
if (!function_exists('fputcsv')) {
  function fputcsv($fp, $line, $separator = ',') {
    for ($i=0; $i < count($line); $i++) {
      if (false !== strpos($line[$i], '"')) {
        $line[$i] = ereg_replace('"', '""',
          $line[$i]);
      }
      if (false !== strpos($line[$i], $separator) ||
          false !== strpos($line[$i], '"')) {
        $line[$i] = '"' . $line[$i] . '"';
      }
    }
```

```php
    fwrite($fp, implode($separator, $line) .
       "\r\n");
  }
}
```

The following code uses our home-grown fputcsv()
to manually create the CSV file that was used
previously.

```php
<?php
  // ...

  $data = array(
    array('April 2005', '19,720,597', '1,310,181'),
    array('January 2005', '18,455,683',
      '1,317,871'),
    array('December 2004', '17,826,404',
      '1,318,739')
  );

  if ($fp = @fopen('usage.csv', 'w')) {
    foreach ($data as $line) {
      fputcsv($fp, $line);
    }
    fclose($fp);
    echo 'CSV written.';
  } else {
    echo 'Cannot open file.';
  }
?>
```

Writing CSV Information (fputcsv.php; excerpt)

USING FILES ON THE SERVER FILE SYSTEM

This code creates the file usage.csv with the following
contents:

```
April 2005,"19,720,597","1,310,181"
January 2005,"18,455,683","1,317,871"
December 2004,"17,826,404","1,318,739"
```

Parsing INI Files

```
parse_ini_file('php.ini', true)
```

Another file format that is very well-known is the INI file format—it was very widely used in the Windows world, but today also drives the configuration of complex software products like PHP. For instance, take a look at php.ini. Here is a (modified) excerpt from the default php.ini that shows very well the structure of INI files:

```
[mail function]
; For Win32 only.
; SMTP = localhost
; For Unix only.  You may supply arguments as well
   (default: "sendmail -t -i").
sendmail_path =
```

So, there are sections that start with a section headline in square brackets, comments that start with a semi-colon, and settings in the format name=value. The PHP function parse_ini_file() now reads in such a PHP file and creates an array out of it: Each section is a sub-array, and within those subarrays you find the names and the values of directives in the INI file. The code at the beginning of this phrase does this (remember to change the path to php.ini, if appropriate), and Figure 6.4 shows the output.

```
<?php
  echo '<xmp>' .
    print_r(parse_ini_file('php.ini', true), true) .
    '</xmp>';
?>
```

Reading Information from INI Files (parse_ini_file.php)

CHAPTER 6

TIP

If you want to avoid the grouping by sections in the INI file, just omit the second parameter parse_ini_file(); then, you get all settings at once.

```
parse_ini_file('php.ini');
```

Figure 6.4 The contents of php.ini as a multidimensional array (parse_ini_file.php; excerpt).

Retrieving File Information

```
$filename = __FILE__;
```

It is rather unusual to use PHP for accessing directory and file information—at least as long as the vast majority of PHP scripts run via HTTP in a web server and not using the command line interface (CLI) or PHP.

However, PHP offers a variety of helper functions that provide information about a file. Most of them are just calling the relevant operating system functions.

```php
<?php
  $filename = __FILE__;
  $data = array(
    'fileatime' => fileatime($filename),
    'filegroup' => filegroup($filename),
    'filemtime' => filemtime($filename),
    'fileowner' => fileowner($filename),
    'filesize' => filesize($filename),
    'is_dir' => var_export(is_dir($filename), true),
    'is_executable' =>
var_export(is_executable($filename), true),
    'is_file' => var_export(is_file($filename),
      true),
    'is_link' => var_export(is_link($filename),
      true),
    'is_readable' => var_export(is_readable
      ($filename), true),
    'is_uploaded_file' => var_export
      (is_uploaded_file($filename), true),
    'is_writable' => var_export
      (is_writable($filename), true)
  );

  echo '<table>';
  foreach ($data as $function => $result) {
    echo
"<tr><td>$function</td><td>$result</td></tr>";
    }
  echo '</table>';
?>
```

Reading Information About Files (fileinfos.php)

The following list shows the most relevant helper functions in this regard:

- fileatime($filename)—Last access to the file
- filegroup($filename)—Group that owns the file
- filemtime($filename)—Last change to the file
- fileowner($filename)—File owner
- filesize($filename)—Size of the file

Another set of helper functions also takes a filename, so the files do not have to be opened before you use these functions:

- is_dir($path)—Whether the path is a directory
- is_executable($filename)—Whether the filename is an executable
- is_file($path)—Whether the path is a (regular) file
- is_link($filename)—Whether the filename is a symbolic link
- is_readable($filename)—Whether the file is readable
- is_uploaded_file($path)—Whether the path is a file uploaded via HTTP (see Chapter 5, "Remembering Users (Cookies and Sessions)")
- is_writable($filename)—Whether the file is writable

Figure 6.5 contains the result of the code at the beginning of this phrase.

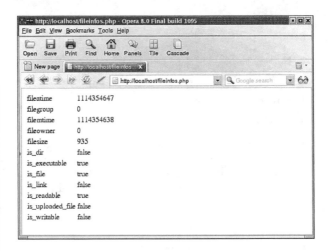

Figure 6.5   Information about the current script
(fileinfos.php).

Copying, Moving, and Deleting Files

```
copy($filename, $tempname1);
rename($tempname1, $tempname2);
unlink($tempname2);
```

Many other standard command-line functions of many
operating systems are available in PHP. This not only
includes chmod() and chgrp(), but also the following
file system operations:

- copy()—Copies a file
- rename()—Moves a file
- unlink()—Deletes a file

The preceding code duplicates the current file, moves it (or renames it), and finally deletes the resulting file.

```php
<?php
  $filename = 'php.ini';
  $tempname1 = $filename . rand();
  $tempname2 = $filename . rand();
  copy($filename, $tempname1);
  echo "Copied to $tempname1<br />";
  rename($tempname1, $tempname2);
  echo "Moved to $tempname2<br />";
  unlink($tempname2);
  echo "File deleted.";
?>
```

Copying, Moving, and Deleting Files (copymovedelete.php)

Browsing the File System

```
$d = dir('.');
while (false !== ($file = $d->read()));
```

Since PHP 3, PHP comes with a built-in class. This sounds strange because OOP (object-oriented programming) did not become "mainstream" in PHP before version 5; however, this special class offers several methods to access the file system. It is possible to get a list of all entries in a directory.

```php
<?php
  $d = dir('.');
  while (false !== ($file = $d->read())) {
    echo htmlspecialchars($file) . '<br />';
  }
  $d->close();
?>
```

Reading a Directory's Contents with PHP's dir Class (dir.php)

You instantiate the class without the keyword new, just by providing the desired path as a parameter. Then the method read() iterates through the list of entries. The preceding code does exactly this and prints out the contents of the current directory.

Note that the two directory entries . (current directory) and .. (parent directory, if you are not in the root directory) are printed out.

Using PHP Streams

In PHP, the concept of PHP streams was introduced. Since then, there is a common denominator for all kinds of resources: files, HTTP and FTP data, and even archive file formats. More about the networking aspect of this can be found in greater detail in Chapter 9, "Communicating with Others;" this chapter just picks out some file-specific features: compression streams.

```php
<?php
  $filename = __FILE__;
  $zipfile = "$filename.zip";

  $data = file_get_contents(__FILE__);
  echo 'Loaded file (size: ' . strlen($data) .
    ').<br />';

  file_put_contents("compress.zlib://$zipfile",
    $data);
  echo 'Zipped file (new size: ' . filesize
    ($zipfile) . ').<br />';

  $data = file_get_contents("compress.zlib://
    $zipfile");
```

CHAPTER 6

```
  echo 'Original file size: ' . strlen($data) .
    '.';
?>
```

Zipping and Unzipping a File (zip.php; excerpt)

One of them can be used to use ZIP files. The pseudo
protocol compress.zlib:// can be used to access ZIP
files as you would access regular files. For this to work,
you have to use the configuration switch –with-gzip
under UNIX/Linux; Windows systems have the
required libraries already included. Then, you can use
the files using, for instance, file_get_contents() and
file_put_contents().

The preceding code loads the current file (with
file_get_contents()), zips it, and writes it to the hard
disk (with file_put_contents()). Then, it reads in the
zipped file (with file_get_contents()) and compares
the file sizes.

When testing this, the code managed to compress the
file from 729 to 336 bytes.

Alternatively, you can use PHP's built-in ZIP functions, which are implemented by a wrapper to the
ZZIPlib library from http://zziplib.sourceforge.net/.
This one can only read data from a ZIP file, unfortunately, but also supports multiple files within an archive
(when using the stream wrapper compress.zlib://, you
first have to tar data to support multiple files).

To install, use extension=php_zip.dll in php.ini under
Windows, or configure PHP with –with-zip, providing
the path to ZZIPlib. The following steps must be taken
to use this extension:

- Open the archive using zip_open()

- Iterate through the archive's entries with `zip_read()`
- Read a specific file using `zip_entry_open()` and `zip_entry_read()`

The following code shows the contents of a ZIP archive and determines the names and file size of all entries.

```php
<?php
  $zipfile = dirname(__FILE__) . '/archive.zip';
  if ($zip = zip_open($zipfile)) {
    while ($file = zip_read($zip)) {
      printf('%s (%d)<br />',
        zip_entry_name($file),
          zip_entry_filesize($file)
      );
    }
    zip_close($zip);
  }
?>
```

Unzipping a File Using ZZIPlib (zziplib.php)

Using Bzip2 Archives

```
file_put_contents("compress.bzip2://$bzip2file",
$data);
```

Another file format that does not come with all operating systems, but offers great compression rates, is Bzip2. Here, PHP also has a built-in stream wrapper: `compress.bzip2://`. To use this, you have to load the Bzip2 library from http://sources.redhat.com/bzip2/. Then use the configuration switch –with-bzip2 (UNIX/Linux), or write `extension=php_bzip2.dll` in your php.ini configuration file (Windows). Then you are ready to go and can compress or decompress files,

as can be seen in the preceding code, which uses
`file_get_contents()` and `file_put_contents()`.

```php
<?php
  $filename = __FILE__;
  $bzip2file = "$filename.bz2";

  $data = file_get_contents(__FILE__);
  echo 'Loaded file (size: ' . strlen($data) .
    ').<br />';

  file_put_contents("compress.bzip2://$bzip2file",
    $data);
  echo 'Bzipped file (new size: ' . filesize
    ($bzip2file) . ').<br />';

  $data = file_get_contents("compress.bzip2://
    $bzip2file");
  echo 'Original file size: ' . strlen($data) . '.';
?>
```

Zipping and Unzipping a File with Bzip2 (bzip2.php; excerpt)

Alternatively, you can use PHP's special Bzip2 functions. They work very similarly to PHP's file functions.
However, for writing, you have to use `bzopen()`,
`bzwrite()`, and `bzclose()` instead of `fopen()`, `fwrite()`,
and `fclose()`, as the following code shows, which
creates a function `file_put_bzip2_contents()`.

```php
<?php
  function file_put_bzip2_contents($filename,
    $content) {
    if ($fp = @bzopen($filename, 'wb')) {
      $result = bzwrite($fp, $content);
      bzclose($fp);
      return $result;
```

```
    } else {
      return false;
    }
  }

  file_put_bzip2_contents('file.txt.bz2',
    "\n-> This text file contains\nsome random text.
      <-");
  echo 'Data written to file.';
?>
```

Zipping a File with BZip2 (bzip2write.php)

The other direction (reading a file from a BZip2 archive)
works analogously to reading a regular file. Instead of
fopen(), fread(), and fclose(), you use bzopen(), bzread(),
and bclose(), as can be seen in the following code, which
writes a function file_get_bzip2_contents().

```
<?php
  function file_get_bzip2_contents($filename) {
    $result = '';
    if ($fp = @bzopen($filename, 'wb')) {
      while ($data = bzread($fp, 4096)) {
        $result .= $data;
      }
      bzclose($fp);
      return $result;
    } else {
      return false;
    }
  }

  echo nl2br(htmlspecialchars(
    file_get_bzip2_contents('file.txt.bz2')
  ));
?>
```

Unzipping a File with BZip2 (bzip2read.php)

Returning Files with an HTTP Request

```
$filename = 'httpfile.zip';
header("Content-Disposition: attachment; filename =
$filename");
```

When a PHP script shall return a (downloadable) file instead of HTML, the correct HTTP headers have to be sent:

- Content-Disposition for the (proposed) name of the file
- Content-Length for the file size
- Content-Type for the MIME type of the file

The preceding code reads in a ZIP file and sends it to the client; Figure 6.6 shows its result in the browser.

```php
<?php
  $filename = 'httpfile.zip';
  $mimetype = 'application/zip';
  $data = file_get_contents($filename);
  $size = strlen($data);
  header("Content-Disposition: attachment; filename
    = $filename");
  header("Content-Length: $size");
  header("Content-Type: $mimetype");
  echo $data;
?>
```

Sending a File with HTTP (httpfile.php)

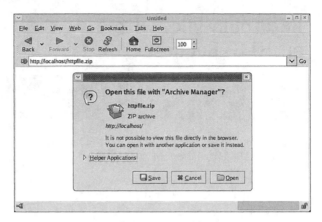

Figure 6.6 The browser wants to save the file.

What Does PEAR Offer?

The following PEAR packages offer functionality that can be used for working with files and streams:

- File offers some helper functions for file access, some of the deprecated to new functionality in more recent PHP releases

- File_Find searches a path for certain files or patterns

- File_SearchReplace does a Search and Replace within files

- Stream_Var allows you to save variables in streams, so you can access them like you would access files or streams

Making Data Dynamic

One of the main strengths of PHP is its support for a vast number of databases. Very often, PHP and MySQL are viewed as an entity. However, other databases have their strengths, too—for instance, it took MySQL a very long time to support features that are considered standard in other systems; however, MySQL is known to be very fast.

This chapter tackles quite a number of databases and shows the basic operations with them: connecting, sending SQL statements, and evaluating the return values. No matter what your database-driven web application must do, it always has to do these steps.

To have some test data, we created a database called phrasebook in the relational database management system (RDBMS) and put a table called quotes in there. This table consists of four fields:

- id—An integer value that is increased by 1 for each new entry entered into the database. Depending on the database system, the data type

is either called IDENTITY, auto_increment, or something similar.

- quote—The quote, as a VARCHAR(255); this length
  works with all systems.

- author—The person who produced the quote, as a
  VARCHAR(50).

- year—The year the quote has been produced
  (sometimes, this is highly speculative), of type INT.

Every database system comes with either management
tools or third-party products available. For instance,
the PHP-based phpMyAdmin (http://www.
phpmyadmin.net/) shown in Figure 7.1 offers very
good access to a MySQL installation.

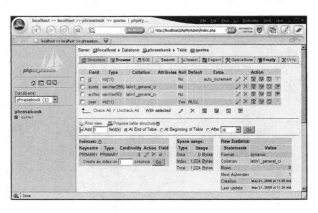

Figure 7.1   Managing a MySQL installation
using phpMyAdmin.

Connecting to MySQL

```
@mysql_connect('localhost', 'user', 'password')
```

Two MySQL extensions for PHP are available. The older one, ext/mysql, was used for PHP 4 and older versions; the newer one, ext/mysqli (the i officially stands for improved, and unofficially for incompatible—but that's cynical), comes with PHP 5 but requires MySQL 4.1 or higher. However, PHP 5 also supports the old extension. Both extensions are covered in this chapter.

```php
<?php
  if ($db = @mysql_connect('localhost', 'user',
    'password')) {
    mysql_select_db('phrasebook', $db);
    echo 'Connected to the database.';
    mysql_close($db);
  } else {
    echo 'Connection failed.';
  }
?>
```

Connecting to MySQL (mysql_connect.php)

To use the extensions, you might have to enable them. Under PHP 4, ext/mysql is automatically activated. Under PHP 5, you have to use extension=php_mysql.dll and also have to copy libmysql.dll to where PHP can find it. If you compile PHP yourself, use the switch –with-mysql=/path/to/mysql for older MySQL versions and ext/mysql.

Now connecting to the database is easy: Just call mysql_connect(), providing the server, username, and

password. You then get a handle that can be used for
mysql_select_db() or to choose a database on the
server. Finally, mysql_close() closes the connection to
the data source.

Connecting to MySQLi

```
@mysqli_connect('localhost', 'user', 'password')
```

If you want to use ext/mysqli, the switch for –with-
mysql has to point to /path/to/mysql_config. Windows
users have to use the files php_mysqli.dll and lib-
mysqli.dll, the rest of the previous install instructions
remain unchanged.

```php
<?php
  if ($db = @mysqli_connect('localhost', 'user',
    'password')) {
    mysqli_select_db($db, 'phrasebook');
    echo 'Connected to the database.';
    mysqli_close($db);
  } else {
    echo 'Connection failed.';
  }
?>
```

Connecting to MySQLi (mysqli_connect.php)

Connecting to MySQL using ext/mysqli works just
like using ext/mysql, however an i is appended to the
function names.

Keep in mind that the different variable order for
mysql(i)_select_db()is one of the prominent differences between the two extensions. The newer one
wants the database handle first. Another difference

between these two extensions is that the database handle is a mandatory parameter whenever used. With ext/mysql, the last handle created by mysql_connect() is the current default handle for the page. One more difference: mysqli_connect() accepts the name of the database as an optional fourth parameter, so you can avoid using mysqli_select_db().

> **NOTE**
>
> Alternatively, the mysqli extension also offers an object-oriented syntax to access a data source. Although this chapter uses the functional approach to make a transition from ext/mysql to ext/mysqli as painless as possible, the following shows what the object-oriented approach looks like:
>
> ```
> $db = new mysqli('localhost', 'user',
>   'password');
> $db->select_db('phrasebook');
> $db->close();
> ```

Sending SQL to MySQL

`mysqli_query()`

The functions mysql_query() and mysqli_query() send SQL to a database identified by a handle—second parameter for mysql_query(), first parameter for mysqli_query(). However, to avoid an attack called "SQL injection" (a method to inject SQL statements using GET or POST data), you absolutely **must** use mysql_real_escape_string() or mysqli_real_escape_ string() to escape any dangerous characters such as single quotes. See the preceding and the following

listing for implementations. The code missing from
those listings (but, of course, it is included in the code
download) is basically an HTML form that accepts a
quote, its author, and a year. Figure 7.2 shows the
HTML input form for the quote collection.

```php
<?php
  if ($db = @mysqli_connect('localhost', 'user',
    'password')) {
    require_once 'stripFormSlashes.inc.php';
    mysqli_select_db($db, 'phrasebook');
    mysqli_query($db, sprintf(
      'INSERT INTO quotes (quote, author, year)
        VALUES (\'%s\', \'%s\', \'%s\')',
      mysqli_real_escape_string($db, $_POST
        ['quote']),
      mysqli_real_escape_string($db, $_POST
        ['author']),
      intval($_POST['year'])));
    echo 'Quote saved.';
    mysqli_close($db);
  } else {
    echo 'Connection failed.';
  }
?>
```

Sending SQL to MySQLi (mysqli_query.php; excerpt)

```php
<?php
  if ($db = @mysql_connect('localhost', 'user',
    'password')) {
    require_once 'stripFormSlashes.inc.php';
    mysql_select_db('phrasebook', $db);
    mysql_query(sprintf(
      'INSERT INTO quotes (quote, author, year)
        VALUES (\'%s\', \'%s\', \'%s\')',
```

```
      mysql_real_escape_string($_POST['quote'],
        $db),
      mysql_real_escape_string($_POST['author'],
        $db),
      intval($_POST['year'])), $db);
    echo 'Quote saved.';
    mysql_close($db);
  } else {
    echo 'Connection failed.';
  }
?>
```

Sending SQL to MySQL (mysql_query.php; excerpt)

Figure 7.2 The HTML input form for
Listings 7.3 and 7.4.

Prepared Statements with MySQL

```
$stmt = mysqli_prepare();
mysqli_stmt_execute($stmt);
```

The new MySQL extension offers a way to both avoid SQL injection and to speed up SQL statements: so-called prepared statements. Within them, you provide placeholders for any dynamic data you are using in the SQL code. You then assign values to those placeholders. The MySQL extension then takes care of all the rest, including escaping of special characters.

```php
<?php
  if ($db = @mysqli_connect('localhost', 'user',
    'password')) {
    require_once 'stripFormSlashes.inc.php';
    mysqli_select_db($db, 'phrasebook');
    $stmt = mysqli_prepare($db, 'INSERT INTO quotes
      (quote, author, year) VALUES (?, ?, ?)');
    $quote = mysqli_real_escape_string($db,
      $_POST['quote']);
    $author = mysqli_real_escape_string($db,
      $_POST['author']);
    $year = intval($_POST['year']);
    mysqli_stmt_bind_param($stmt, 'ssi', $quote,
      $author, $year);
    if (mysqli_stmt_execute($stmt)) {
      echo 'Quote saved.';
    } else {
      echo 'Error writing quote.';
    }
    mysqli_close($db);
  } else {
    echo 'Connection failed.';
  }
?>
```

Using Prepared Statements with MySQL (mysqli_stmt_execute.php; excerpt)

So first, you prepare an SQL statement with
mysqli_prepare(); as a placeholder character, you use a
question mark:

```
$stmt = mysqli_prepare($db, 'INSERT INTO quotes
  (quote, author, year) VALUES (?, ?, ?)');
```

Then, you bind values to each parameter. First, you
provide the statement returned by mysqli_prepare, then
one-character codes for the values of all parameters (s
for string, i for integer, d for double). Finally, you
provide a list of values. Because these values are used
by reference, you have to provide variables, not raw
values.

```
mysqli_stmt_bind_param($stmt, 'ssi', $quote,
  $author, $year);
```

Finally, mysqli_stmt_execute() executes the prepared
statement.

> **NOTE**
>
> The ext/mysqli extension supports some of the new fea-
> tures or recent MySQL versions, including transactions. For
> this, the following functions are available:
>
> - mysqli_autocommit($db, false) deactivates
>   autocommit
> - mysqli_rollback($db) rolls back all pending
>   transactions
> - mysqli_commit($db) commits all pending
>   transactions

> **TIP**
>
> When using auto_increment values, the functions mysql_insert_id() and mysqli_insert_id() return the value of the auto_increment field of the last INSERT SQL statement created.

Retrieving Results of a Query to MySQL

```
$result = mysqli_query(query);
mysql fetch object($result);
```

The return value of mysql_query() or mysqli_query() is a pointer to the actual resultset. It can be used to iterate through the complete list of entries returned by a SELECT statement. For this, these functions come in handy:

- mysql_fetch_assoc() and mysqli_fetch_assoc() return the current row in the resultset as an associative array (field names become keys) and move farther to the next row.

- mysql_fetch_object() and mysqli_fetch_object() return the current row in the resultset as an object (field names become properties) and move farther to the next row.

- mysql_fetch_row() and mysqli_fetch_row() return the current row in the resultset as a numeric array and move farther to the next row.

```
<table>
<tr><th>#</th><th>Quote</th><th>Author</th><th>Year
  </th></tr>
<?php
  if ($db = @mysqli_connect('localhost', 'user',
    'password')) {
    mysqli_select_db($db, 'phrasebook');
    $result = mysqli_query($db, 'SELECT * FROM
      quotes');
    while ($row = mysqli_fetch_object($result)) {
      printf(
'<tr><td>%s</td><td>%s</td><td>%s</td><td>%s</td></
  tr>',
        htmlspecialchars($row->id),
        htmlspecialchars($row->quote),
        htmlspecialchars($row->author),
        htmlspecialchars($row->year)
      );
    }
    mysqli_close($db);
  } else {
    echo '<tr><td colspan="4">Connection failed.
      </td></tr>';
  }
?>
</table>
```

Retrieving Data from MySQL (mysqli_fetch.php; excerpt)

There are other functions, as well; however, these three
are the ones that are used more often. The following
code uses mysql_fetch_assoc(), whereas the preceding
listing prints out the contents of the database table
with mysqli_fetch_object(). The main idea is to use a
while loop—all mysql_fetch_*/mysqli_fetch_* functions return false when no data is left in the resultset.

```
<table>
<tr><th>#</th><th>Quote</th><th>Author</th><th>Year<
   /th></tr>
<?php
  if ($db = @mysql_connect('localhost', 'user',
    'password')) {
    mysql_select_db('phrasebook', $db);
    $result = mysql_query('SELECT * FROM quotes',
      $db);
    while ($row = mysql_fetch_assoc($result)) {
      printf(
'<tr><td>%s</td><td>%s</td><td>%s</td><td>%s</td></
  tr>',
        htmlspecialchars($row['id']),
        htmlspecialchars($row['quote']),
        htmlspecialchars($row['author']),
        htmlspecialchars($row['year'])
      );
    }
    mysql_close($db);
  } else {
    echo '<tr><td colspan="4">Connection failed.
      </td></tr>';
  }
?>
</table>
```

Retrieving Data from MySQL (mysql_fetch.php; excerpt)

Figure 7.3 shows the contents of the database after some (political) quotes have been filled in. Sorry, I am from abroad—I took the first ones I found.

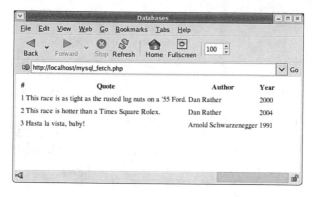

Figure 7.3 The contents of the database.

Connecting to SQLite

```
@sqlite_open('quotes.db', 0666, $error)
```

Starting with PHP 5, SQLite is bundled with the scripting language. This is a lightweight, file-based database. That allows very fast reading (in many cases, even faster than when using a "real" database), but writing can sometimes take longer than with other systems because file locking is an issue. However, PHP 4 users can also use SQLite as there is a PECL (PHP Extension Community Library) module available at http://pecl.php.net/.

```php
<?php
  if ($db = @sqlite_open('quotes.db', 0666, $error))
    {
    echo 'Connected to the database.';
    sqlite_close($db);
  } else {
```

```
    echo 'Connection failed: ' . htmlspecialchars
      ($error);
  }
?>
```

Connecting to SQLite (sqlite_open.php)

If you use PHP 5, SQLite support is already included; when using PHP 4, use pear install SQLite or, when Windows is the operating system of your choice, load the current SQLite binary extension at http://snaps.php.net/win32/PECL_STABLE/php_sqlite.dll, copy it to PHP's extension folder, and then load it using extension=php_sqlite.dll in your php.ini.

Then, you can connect to a SQLite data source using sqlite_open(). As the first parameter, you provide the name of the database file (it gets created if it doesn't exist yet). For this to work, the PHP process needs read and write privileges to the file. The second parameter is the file open mode (0666 is recommended); however, as of this writing, this parameter is ignored. The second parameter is a variable that contains any error messages (such as insufficient rights).

NOTE

Just like ext/mysqli, the SQLite extension under PHP 5 can also be accessed using an object-oriented programming (OOP) approach:

```
<?php
  $db = new SQLiteDatabase('quotes.db');
  echo 'Connected to the database.';
  $db->close();
?>
```

For the sake of backward compatibility, this chapter uses the functional approach for the subsequent phrases.

Sending SQL to SQLite

sqlite_exec()

The PHP function sqlite_exec() sends an SQL
statement to the database. As the first parameter, the
database handle—returned by sqlite_open()—is used;
the second parameter is the SQL string. To avoid SQL
injection, the PHP function sqlite_escape_string()
escapes dangerous characters in dynamic data. The preceding code implements this for the sample table
quotes that has also been used in the MySQL phrases.

```php
<?php
  if ($db = @sqlite_open('quotes.db', 0666, $error))
  {
  require_once 'stripFormSlashes.inc.php';
  sqlite_exec($db, sprintf(
    'INSERT INTO quotes (quote, author, year)
       VALUES (\'%s\', \'%s\', \'%s\')',
    sqlite_escape_string($_POST['quote']),
    sqlite_escape_string($_POST['author']),
    intval($_POST['year'])));
  echo 'Quote saved.';
  sqlite_close($db);
  } else {
  echo 'Connection failed: ' . htmlspecialchars
    ($error);
  }
?>
```

Sending SQL to SQLite (sqlite_exec.php; excerpt)

MAKING DATA DYNAMIC

> **TIP**
>
> If a table contains an identity column (data type
> `INTEGER PRIMARY KEY` when using SQLite), calling
> `sqlite_last_insert_rowid()` after sending an SQL
> statement returns the value this column has for the new
> entry in the database.

Retrieving Results of a Query to SQLite

```
$result = sqlite_query($db, 'SELECT * FROM quotes');
sqlite_fetch_array($result);
```

The function `sqlite_exec()` from the previous phrase
is very quick performing; however, it is not possible to
access return values from the SQL statement sent with
it. For this, `sqlite_query()` must be used. This function
returns a handle of the resultset of the query. The following functions can then be used to iterate over the
resultset:

- `sqlite_fetch_arrray()` returns the current row in
  the resultset as an associative array (field names
  become keys) and moves farther to the next row.

- `sqlite_fetch_object()` returns the current row in
  the resultset as an object (field names become
  properties) and moves farther to the next row.

- `sqlite_fetch_all()` returns the complete resultset
  as an array of associative arrays.

```
<table>
<tr><th>#</th><th>Quote</th><th>Author</th><th>Year<
   /th></tr>
<?php
  if ($db = @sqlite_open('quotes.db', 0666, $error))
    {
    $result = sqlite_query($db, 'SELECT * FROM
      quotes');
    while ($row = sqlite_fetch_array($result)) {
      printf(
'<tr><td>%s</td><td>%s</td><td>%s</td><td>%s</td></
   tr>',
        htmlspecialchars($row['id']),
        htmlspecialchars($row['quote']),
        htmlspecialchars($row['author']),
        htmlspecialchars($row['year'])
      );
    }
    sqlite_close($db);
  } else {
    printf('<tr><td colspan="4">Connection failed:
      %s</td></tr>',
      htmlspecialchars($error));
  }
?>
</table>
```

Retrieving Data from SQLite (sqlite_fetch.php; excerpt)

The preceding listing shows how to access all data
within the resultset using sqlite_fetch_array(). A
while loop calls this function as long as it returns
something other than false (which means that there is
no data left).

> **TIP**
>
> Using `sqlite_fetch_all()` reads the whole resultset into memory at once. So, if you do not have much data, this is the best-performing method. If you have more data, an iterative approach using `sqlite_fetch_array()` and `sqlite_fetch_object()` might be better.

Connecting to PostgreSQL

`@pg_connect()`

PostgreSQL has a growing fanbase. Some even say this is because the new version 8.0 finally comes in a native Windows version. However, most productive systems that use PostgreSQL are hosted on Linux or UNIX, nevertheless.

After installing the database, web-based administration software such as phpPgAdmin (http://sourceforge.net/projects/phppgadmin) or other tools such as the graphical user interface (GUI) application pgAdmin (http://www.pgadmin.org/) can be used to administer the database. Alternatively, the command-line tool can be used. To allow PHP to access the PostgreSQL installation, Windows users must load the extension with the entry extension(`php_pgsql.dll`) in `php.ini`; UNIX/Linux users configure PHP with the switch `-with-pgsql=/path/to/pgsql`.

Then, `pg_connect()` connects to the data source. You have to provide a connection string that contains all important data, including host, port, name of the database, and user credentials.

```php
<?php
  if ($db = @pg_connect('host=localhost port=5432
  dbname=phrasebook user=postgres password=
  abc123')) {
    echo 'Connected to the database.';
    pg_close($db);
  } else {
    echo 'Connection failed.';
  }
?>
```

Connecting to PostgreSQL (pg_connect.php)

Sending SQL to PostgreSQL

pg_query()

The function pg_query() sends SQL to the
PostgreSQL installation. Again, escaping potentially
dangerous characters such as single quotes is a must;
this can be done with the pg_escape_string() function. In this code, you see the PHP portion of the
script that accepts funny (or not-so-funny) phrases in
an HTML form and writes it to the database.

```php
<?php
  if ($db = @pg_connect('host=localhost port=5432
    dbname=phrasebook user=postgres
    password=abc123')) {
    require_once 'stripFormSlashes.inc.php';
    pg_query($db, sprintf(
      'INSERT INTO quotes (quote, author, year)
        VALUES (\'%s\', \'%s\', \'%s\')',
      pg_escape_string($_POST['quote']),
      pg_escape_string($_POST['author']),
```

```
    intval($_POST['year'])));
  echo 'Quote saved.';
  pg_close($db);
} else {
  echo 'Connection failed.';
}
?>
```

Sending SQL to PostgreSQL (pg_query.php; excerpt)

NOTE

Retrieving the value in the identity column after the last
INSERT statement is a bit tricky. The PostgreSQL term for
such a data type is SERIAL, which automatically creates a
sequence. To get the sequence's value, you can use
pg_last_oid() to retrieve the oid (object id) of this
value. Then, execute a SELECT id FROM quotes WHERE
oid=<oid>, when <oid> is the oid you just retrieved. This
finally returns the desired value.

Updating Data in PostgreSQL

pg_insert()

Another way to insert or update data in PostgreSQL
comes in the form of the functions pg_insert() and
pg_update(). The first parameter must be the database
handle, the second parameter is the table to be inserted
into/updated, and the third parameter contains some
data in the form of an associative array (column names
are the keys). In the event of an UPDATE SQL statement,
the update condition must also be submitted as an
array in the fourth parameter of the function. The preceding code shows how to insert data.

```php
<?php
  if ($db = @pg_connect('host=localhost port=5432
    dbname=phrasebook user=postgres
    password=abc123')) {
    require_once 'stripFormSlashes.inc.php';
    $data = array(
      'quote' => pg_escape_string($_POST['quote']),
      'author' => pg_escape_string($_POST
        ['author']),
      'year' => intval($_POST['year'])
    );
    pg_insert($db, 'quotes', $data);
    echo 'Quote saved.';
    pg_close($db);
  } else {
    echo 'Connection failed.';
  }
?>
```

Sending SQL to PostgreSQL (pg_insert.php; excerpt)

Retrieving Results of a Query to PostgreSQL

```
$result = pg_query();
pg_fetch_row($result);
```

The return value of a call to pg_query() is a pointer to a resultset that can be used with these functions:

- pg_fetch_assoc() returns the current row in the resultset as an associative array

- pg_fetch_object() returns the current row in the resultset as an object

- pg_fetch_row() returns the current row in the resultset as a numeric array

- pg_fetch_all() returns the complete resultset as an array of associative arrays

```
<table>
<tr><th>#</th><th>Quote</th><th>Author</th><th>Year<
  /th></tr>
<?php
  if ($db = @pg_connect('host=localhost port=5432
    dbname=phrasebook user=postgres
    password=abc123')) {
    $result = pg_query($db, 'SELECT * FROM quotes');
    while ($row = pg_fetch_row($result)) {
      vprintf(
 '<tr><td>%s</td><td>%s</td><td>%s</td><td>%s</td></
    tr>',
        $row
      );
    }
    pg_close($db);
  } else {
    echo '<tr><td colspan="4">Connection
failed.</td></tr>';
  }
?>
</table>
```

Retrieving Data from PostgreSQL (pg_fetch.php; excerpt)

The code uses pg_fetch_row() to read out all data from the quotes table.

Alternatively, pg_select() works similarly to pg_insert() and pg_update(). Just provide a database handle, a table name, and maybe a WHERE clause in the form of an array, and you get the complete resultset as an array of (associative) arrays.

```
$data = pg_select($db, 'quotes');
```

Connecting to Oracle

`@oci_connect()`

Two PHP extensions are available for Oracle, but only one is actively maintained and also works with more recent versions of the RDBMS. To install it, configure PHP with the switch --with-oci8. The environment variable ORACLE_HOME must be set so that PHP can find the client libraries. Windows users need the php.ini directive extension=php_oci8.dll. In addition, PHP requires read access to the client libraries. Then, oci_connect() tries to establish a connection to the server. The order of the parameters is a bit strange: first username and password, then the name of the service (that has been configured using the configuration assistant or is part of the tnsnames.ora file). The return value is a handle to the connection and is required by further operations in the database.

```php
<?php
  if ($db = @oci_connect('scott', 'tiger', 'orcl'))
    {
    echo 'Connected to the database.';
    oci_close($db);
  } else {
    echo 'Connection failed.';
  }
?>
```

Connecting to Oracle (oci_connect.php)

MAKING DATA DYNAMIC

WARNING

In PHP 4, oci_connect() did not exist yet, so for this version, ocilogon() has to be used. However, this is considered deprecated in PHP 5. Therefore, all Oracle phrases in this chapter use the PHP 5 syntax; however, files with the extension .php4 are included in the download repository that work on older PHP versions.

Sending SQL to Oracle

oci_execute()

This section again uses the quotes table, which also includes an identity column; however, this is a bit more complicated to implement with Oracle. Refer to the script quotes.oracle.sql in the download archive for more information.

```php
<?php
  if ($db = @oci_connect('scott', 'tiger', 'orcl'))
    {
    require_once 'stripFormSlashes.inc.php';
    $sql = 'INSERT INTO quotes (quote, author, year)
      VALUES (:quote, :author, :year)';
    $stmt = oci_parse($db, $sql);
    oci_bind_by_name($stmt, ':quote',
      $_POST['quote']);
    oci_bind_by_name($stmt, ':author',
      $_POST['author']);
    oci_bind_by_name($stmt, ':year',
      intval($_POST['year']));
    oci_execute($stmt, OCI_COMMIT_ON_SUCCESS);
    echo 'Quote saved.';
    oci_close($db);
```

```
  } else {
    echo 'Connection failed.';
  }
?>
```

Sending SQL to Oracle (oci_execute.php; excerpt)

To send SQL to Oracle, two steps are required. First, a call to oci_parse() parses an SQL string and returns a resource that can then be executed using oci_execute(). The second parameter of oci_execute() is quite important. Several constants are allowed, but most of the time, OCI_DEFAULT is used. Despite the name, that's not the default value, but means "no auto-commit." On the other hand, OCI_COMMIT_ON_SUCCESS commits the pending transaction when no error has occurred. And this is, indeed, the default value.

Unfortunately, there is no such thing as oci_escape_string() to escape special characters for use in an SQL statement. Therefore, prepared statements are a must—but are also very easy to implement. For this, the SQL statement must contain placeholders that start with a colon:

```
$sql = 'INSERT INTO quotes (quote, author, year)
  VALUES (:quote, :author, :year)';
```

Then, these placeholders have to be filled with values. For this, oci_bind_by_name() must be used:

```
oci_bind_by_name($stmt, ':quote', $_POST['quote']);
```

The preceding code sends some form data to the database. No worries about special characters because oci_bind_by_name takes care of that.

> **NOTE**
>
> When you are using OCI_DEFAULT as the commit mode, the changes must be written to the database using oci_commit($db); oci_rollback($db) performs a rollback.

> **TIP**
>
> By the way, if you want to retrieve the autovalue of the most recent INSERT operation, you have to do it within a transaction and execute SELECT quotes_id.CURVAL AS id FROM DUAL, where quotes_id is the name of the sequence you are using.

Retrieving Results of a Query to Oracle

oci fetch_object($stmt)

You have several ways to access the return values of an SQL query, but the following functions are used most often in practice:

- oci_fetch_assoc() returns the current row in the resultset as an associative array.

- oci_fetch_object() returns the current row in the resultset as an object.

- oci_fetch_row() returns the current row in the resultset as a numeric array.

- oci_fetch_all() returns the complete resultset as an array of associative arrays. However, five parameters are required: the statement object from oci_parse(), the array that is used for the return data, the number of lines to skip, the maximum number of rows to be returned (-1 means infinite), and whether to return a numeric (OCI_NUM) or associative (OCI_ASSOC) array.

The listing in this phrase uses a while loop and oci_fetch_object() to retrieve all data in the table.

```
<table>
<tr><th>#</th><th>Quote</th><th>Author</th><th>Year<
  /th></tr>
<?php
  if ($db = @oci_connect('scott', 'tiger', 'orcl'))
    {
    $stmt = oci_parse($db, 'SELECT * FROM quotes');
    oci_execute($stmt, OCI_COMMIT_ON_SUCCESS);
    while ($row = oci_fetch_object($stmt)) {
      printf(
'<tr><td>%s</td><td>%s</td><td>%s</td><td>%s</td></
  tr>',
        htmlspecialchars($row->ID),
        htmlspecialchars($row->QUOTE),
        htmlspecialchars($row->AUTHOR),
        htmlspecialchars($row->YEAR)
      );
    }
    oci_close($db);
  } else {
    echo '<tr><td colspan="4">Connection
      failed.</td></tr>';
  }
?>
</table>
```

Retrieving Data from Oracle (oci_fetch.php; excerpt)

> **NOTE**
>
> Oracle always returns column names in uppercase.
> Therefore, you have to use uppercase object properties or
> uppercase associative array keys when accessing the return
> values of an SQL query.

Connecting to MSSQL

`@mssql_connect()`

The Microsoft SQL engine comes in two flavors: the
fully featured (and fully priced) Microsoft SQL Server
(short: MSSQL) and the free edition, the Microsoft
SQL Server Desktop Engine (short: MSDE), available
for free at http://www.asp.net/msde/. Both versions
are supported by PHP because they are compatible
to each other. To make it work, you need the line
`extension=php_mssql.dll` in your `php.ini`. Also, PHP
needs access to the client libraries for MSSQL/MSDE,
the file `ntwdblib.dll`. In PHP 5, this file is in the PHP
directory, so the PHP process just needs read access to
it. In PHP 4, you might have to copy the file (that
resides in the `dll` subdirectory) somewhere else, for
example in the Windows `system32` folder.

However, UNIX/Linux systems can also connect to
MSSQL/MSDE installations in a heterogenous network, a combination that powers some high-traffic
websites. For this to work, you have to download the
FreeTDS library from http://www.freetds.org/ and
install it after unpacking the distribution with this
command:

```
./configure –prefix=/usr/local/tds –with-tdsver= 4.2
make
sudo make install
```

CHAPTER 7

Then, reconfigure PHP with the switch –with-sybase=/usr/local/freetds.

Finally, you can connect to the server using mssql_connect() and select the database to be used using mssql_select_db(), as the preceding listing shows.

```php
<?php
  if ($db = @mssql_connect('localhost', 'user',
    'password')) {
    mssql_select_db('phrasebook');
    echo 'Connected to the database.';
    mssql_close($db);
  } else {
    echo 'Connection failed.';
  }
?>
```

Connecting to MSSDE/MSDE (mssql_connect.php)

MSSQL/MSDE supports two modes to authenticate users: SQL authentication and Windows authentication. The latter one checks whether the current Windows user has sufficient rights to access the database. In a controlled environment, this might be a better idea than using username and password. However, you first have to find out which user is used. For instance, Microsoft IIS web server software uses the Internet guest account, that is, IUSR_<machinename>. Therefore, this user requires privileges in the database.

To use Windows authentication—sometimes also called trusted connection—you need the following php.ini directive:

```
mssql.secure_connection = On
```

Sending SQL to MSSQL

mssql_query()

The function mssql_query() sends an SQL statement to the MSSQL/MSDE installation. Again, the parameter order is a bit strange: first the SQL command, then the database handle. However, as you saw in the previous listing in the call to mssql_select_db(), this information can also be omitted—then, the last connection established is used automatically.

Another important point is escaping special characters. In MSSQL/MSDE, single quotes must not be escaped using a backslash, but double quotes are the way to go:

```
INSERT INTO quotes (quote, author, year) VALUES
('Ain''t Misbehavin''', 'Louis Armstrong', 1929)
```

To achieve this, addslashes() can be used—however, first, it has to be configured to behave so that MSSQL/MSDE-compatible strings are returned:

```
ini_set('magic_quotes_sybase', 'On');
$author = addslashes($_POST['author']);
```

```php
<?php
  if ($db = @mssql_connect('localhost', 'user',
    'password')) {
    require_once 'stripFormSlashes.inc.php';
    mssql_select_db('phrasebook', $db);
    ini_set('magic_quotes_sybase', 'On');
    mssql_query(sprintf(
      'INSERT INTO quotes (quote, author, year)
        VALUES (\'%s\', \'%s\', \'%s\')',
      addslashes($_POST['quote']),
      addslashes($_POST['author']),
```

```
      intval($_POST['year'])), $db);
    echo 'Quote saved.';
    mssql_close($db);
  } else {
    echo 'Connection failed.';
  }
?>
```

Sending SQL to MSSQL/MSDE (mssql_execute.php; excerpt)

The listing at the beginning of this phrase sanitizes some form data and writes it to the (by now) well-known sample database.

Retrieving Results of a Query to MSSQL

```
$result = mssql_query();
mssql_fetch_assoc($result);
```

Finally, there is, of course, also a way to retrieve all data in the resultset. A while loop comes into play, using one of these functions:

- mssql_fetch_assoc() returns the current row in the resultset as an associative array
- mssql_fetch_object() returns the current row in the resultset as an object
- mssql_fetch_row() returns the current row in the resultset as a numeric array

MAKING DATA DYNAMIC

```
<table>
<tr><th>#</th><th>Quote</th><th>Author</th><th>Year<
  /th></tr>
<?php
  if ($db = @mssql_connect('localhost', 'user',
    'password')) {
    mssql_select_db('phrasebook', $db);
    $result = mssql_query('SELECT * FROM quotes',
      $db);
    while ($row = mssql_fetch_assoc($result)) {
      printf(
'<tr><td>%s</td><td>%s</td><td>%s</td><td>%s</td></
  tr>',
        htmlspecialchars($row['id']),
        htmlspecialchars($row['quote']),
        htmlspecialchars($row['author']),
        htmlspecialchars($row['year'])
      );
    }
    mssql_close($db);
  } else {
    echo '<tr><td colspan="4">Connection
      failed.</td></tr>';
  }
?>
</table>
```

Retrieving Data from MSSQL/MSDE (mssql_fetch.php; excerpt)

Connecting to Firebird

ibase_connect()

The Firebird database is currently more an insider's tip than a widely in use database, but is getting more users and may be an alternative to established RDBMS. The origins of this database lie in Borland's InterBase product. Therefore, the extension is called ibase or interbase. So, Windows users need extension= php_interbase.dll in their php.ini, whereas "self-compilers" must configure PHP with the switch --with-interbase=/path/to/firebird. Then, Firebird supports two modes: a file mode comparable to SQLite and a server mode. For the sake of interoperability and for an easy deployment, this section uses the file mode.

```php
<?php
  if ($db =
ibase_connect('localhost:/tmp/quotes.gdb', 'user',
  'password')) {
    echo 'Connected to the database.';
    ibase_close($db);
  } else {
    echo 'Connection failed.';
  }
?>
```

Connecting to InterBase/Firebird (ibase_connect.php)

This section also uses .gdb files that are compatible with both Firebird and Interbase; the new Firebird format has the extension .fdb. After this file is created, ibase_connect() connects to the file or database. For the host, you have to provide a string in the format `'localhost:/path/to/file.gdb'` when using TCP/IP, or the local filename (the listings assume that the file resides in /tmp on the local machine); you also need a username and a password.

Sending SQL to Firebird

`ibase_execute()`

The function ibase_query() can be used to send an SQL string to the database. However, there is no ibase_escape_string(); so, to be safe from SQL injection, a prepared statement must be used. Here, the function ibase_prepare() comes into play: It parses an SQL statement (with question marks as placeholders) and returns a statement object. Then, ibase_execute() executes this statement and retrieves the values for the placeholders as additional parameters.

```php
<?php
  if ($db =
ibase_connect('localhost:/tmp/quotes.gdb', 'user',
  'password')) {
    require_once 'stripFormSlashes.inc.php';
    $sql = 'INSERT INTO quotes (id, quote, author,
      qyear) ' .
      'VALUES (GEN_ID(quotes_gen, 1), ?, ?, ?)';
    $stmt = ibase_prepare($db, $sql);
    ibase_execute($stmt,
      $_POST['quote'], $_POST['author'], intval
        ($_POST['year']));
    echo 'Quote saved.';
    ibase_close($db);
```

```
  } else {
    echo 'Connection failed.';
  }
?>
```

Sending SQL to InterBase/Firebird (ibase_execute.php; excerpt)

NOTE

The preceding code contains two specialities of Firebird. First, the identity column is driven by a generator in the database; the call to GEN_ID(quotes_gen, 1) enters the next available value in this column when inserting a new field. Also, the word year is reserved within Firebird, so the column's name is qyear.

Retrieving Results of a Query to Firebird

```
$result = ibase_query();
ibase_fetch_object($result);
```

No matter if you are using ibase_query or ibase_execute(), at the end, you have a handle for the resultset, which you can iterate with ibase_fetch_assoc()—which returns an associative array—or ibase_fetch_object()—which returns an object. This code uses the latter method.

Keep in mind that Firebird and InterBase return column names in uppercase, so the object properties (and the keys in the associative arrays) are uppercase, too.

MAKING DATA DYNAMIC

```
<table>
<tr><th>#</th><th>Quote</th><th>Author</th><th>Year<
  /th></tr>
<?php
  if ($db = ibase_connect('//CHRISTIAN2003/tmp/
    quotes.gdb', 'user', 'password')) {
    $result = ibase_query($db, 'SELECT * FROM
      quotes');
    while ($row = ibase_fetch_object($result)) {
      printf(
'<tr><td>%s</td><td>%s</td><td>%s</td><td>%s</td></
  tr>',
        htmlspecialchars($row->ID),
        htmlspecialchars($row->QUOTE),
        htmlspecialchars($row->AUTHOR),
        htmlspecialchars($row->QYEAR)
      );
    }
    ibase_close($db);
  } else {
    echo '<tr><td colspan="4">Connection
      failed.</td></tr>';
  }
?>
</table>
```

Retrieving Data from InterBase/Firebird (ibase_fetch.php; excerpt)

Connecting Via PDO

```
try {
  $db = new PDO('sqlite:PDOquotes.db');
}
```

Finally, a new development from some core PHP developers and one of the key features of PHP 5.1 is PDO, short for PHP Data Objects. There are several abstraction classes in PHP, but PDO will become the official one.

PDO is already available in PEAR, at http://pecl.php.net/package/PDO. UNIX/Linux users can install it using `pear install PDO` or by compiling it manually; Windows users have to refer to http://pec14win.php.net/list.php/5_0 for PHP 5.0.x, and to http://pec14win.php.net/list.php/5_1 for PHP 5.1. Then, `extension=php_pdo.dll` (or `extension=pdo.so` on other systems) in `php.ini` does the trick.

```php
<?php
  try {
    $db = new PDO('sqlite:PDOquotes.db');
    echo 'Connected to the database.';
  } catch (PDOException $ex) {
    echo 'Connection failed: ' .
htmlspecialchars($ex->getMessage());
  }
?>
```

Connecting Via PDO (pdo_connect.php)

After installing PDO, a driver for the database to be used must be loaded, as well. As of this writing, the following drivers are available:

- PDO_FIREBIRD for InterBase/Firebird
- PDO_MYSQL for MySQL 3.x and 4.0
- PDO_OCI for Oracle
- PDO_ODBC for ODBC and IBM's DB2
- PDO_PGSQL for PostgreSQL
- PDO_SQLITE for SQLite

To make this as portable and easy to deploy as possible, the following phrases use the SQLite driver; however, other drivers and database systems are just as good. Note that this driver uses SQLite 3 and not SQLite 2 as bundled with PHP 5 (that's why the binary distribution of the driver weighs in at over 200KB). Whatever system you choose, download and install the driver and load it **after** PDO in your php.ini.

Because PDO only works with PHP 5 and later versions, you can use an object-oriented approach. All you need is a suitable data source name (DSN), a user, and a password (and possibly other options). The preceding code connects to/creates an SQLite file.

Sending SQL Via PDO

```
$stmt = $db->prepare($sql);
$stmt->execute();
```

To send SQL via PDO, a statement must be executed using the query() method. As always, you need a way to escape special characters. This can, once again, be done using prepared statements. First, an SQL query can be parsed using a method called prepare(), whereas placeholders start with a colon. Then, the bindParam() method binds a value to a placeholder name. Finally, the execute() method sends the statement to the database.

```
<?php
  try {
    $db = new PDO('sqlite:PDOquotes.db');
    require_once 'stripFormSlashes.inc.php';
    $sql = 'INSERT INTO quotes (quote, author, year)
```

```
   VALUES (:quote, :author, :year)';
  $stmt = $db->prepare($sql);
  $stmt->bindParam(':quote', $_POST['quote']);
  $stmt->bindParam(':author', $_POST['author']);
  $stmt->bindParam(':year',
    intval($_POST['year']));
  $stmt->execute();
  echo 'Quote saved.';
} catch (PDOException $ex) {
  echo 'Connection failed: ' . htmlspecialchars
    ($ex->getMessage());
}
?>
```

Sending SQL Via PDO (pdo_execute.php; excerpt)

Retrieving Results of a Query Via PDO

```
$result = $db->query();
$result->fetch(PDO::FETCH_ASSOC);
```

Finally, reading out results from an SQL query with PDO is done using the standard approach: Send the SELECT query to the server and then use a while loop to iterate over the results. Here, the iteration is done using the fetch() method. As a parameter, you can provide constants such as PDO::FETCH_ASSOC (which returns an associative array) or PDO::FETCH_OBJ (which returns an object). Alternatively, you can use the fetchAll() method and get an array of arrays, so you have all the data at once.

This code uses fetch() and PDO::FETCH_ASSOC to read out all data from the data source.

```
<table>
<tr><th>#</th><th>Quote</th><th>Author</th><th>Year<
  /th></tr>
<?php
  try {
    $db = new PDO('sqlite:PDOquotes.db');
    $result = $db->query('SELECT * FROM quotes');
    while ($row = $result->fetch(PDO::FETCH_ASSOC)) {
      printf(

'<tr><td>%s</td><td>%s</td><td>%s</td><td>%s</td></
  tr>',
        htmlspecialchars($row['id']),
        htmlspecialchars($row['quote']),
        htmlspecialchars($row['author']),
        htmlspecialchars($row['year'])
      );
    }
  } catch (PDOException $ex) {
    echo 'Connection failed: ' . htmlspecialchars
      ($ex->getMessage());
  }
?>
</table>
```

Retrieving Data Via PDO (pdo_fetch.php; excerpt)

NOTE

As of this writing, PDO cannot be considered as stable yet; therefore, it is possible that the application programming interface (API) or behavior of PDO may change in the future. Also, if you try out PDO, be aware that this is still not proven to be as reliable as PHP itself.

What Does PEAR Offer?

The following PEAR packages (among others) offer database abstraction layers and other goodies for database access:

- DB is the best-known database abstraction layer in PEAR
- DB_DataObject can create SQL from objects
- DB_QueryTool offers some help for building SQL queries
- MDB and MDB2 are also feature-rich database abstraction layers

8

Using XML

After the hype, the Extensible Markup Language (XML) is now really used almost everywhere. An application that receives a lot of buzz is Web Services, a technology that is covered in detail in Chapter 9, "Communicating with Others." However, XML can be used elsewhere, as well. It is a good format to store any kind of data.

The tasks behind using XML are always the same: reading data from XML and writing data into it. So this chapter focuses on these tasks and shows how to implement them.

Unfortunately, PHP 4's XML support was somewhat limited. Some extensions did not prove to be very stable. This changed drastically with PHP 5 and a revamped XML support. Therefore, the main focus of this chapter is on PHP 4. In PHP 5.1, some new features will be added that are already covered in this chapter.

As the sample XML file and format in this chapter, the XML from the following code reuses the quotes database example from the previous chapter. As you can see, `<quotes>` is the root element, and each quote (including its author and the year the phrase was coined) is contained in a <quote> element.

```xml
<?xml version="1.0" encoding="ISO-8859-1" ?>
<quotes>
  <quote year="1991">
    <phrase>Hasta la vista, baby!</phrase>
    <author>Arnold Schwarzenegger</author>
  </quote>
</quotes>
```

The sample XML file (quotes.xml; excerpt)

Parsing XML with SAX

`$sax = xml_parser_create();`

SAX is an approach to parse XML documents, but not to validate them. The good thing is that you can use it with both PHP 4 and PHP 5 with no changes. In PHP 4, the SAX parsing is already available on all platforms, so no separate installation is necessary.

```php
<?php
  // ...
  $sax = xml_parser_create();
  xml_parser_set_option($sax, XML_OPTION_CASE_
    FOLDING, false);
  xml_parser_set_option($sax, XML_OPTION_SKIP_WHITE,
    true);
  xml_set_element_handler($sax, 'sax_start',
    'sax_end');
  xml_set_character_data_handler($sax, 'sax_cdata');
  xml_parse($sax, file_get_contents('quotes.xml'),
    true);
  xml_parser_free($sax);
?>
```

Parsing XML with SAX (sax.php; excerpt)

You create a SAX (Simple API for XML) parser using
xml_parser_create(). This parser can look at an XML
file and react upon various events. The following three
events are the most important ones:

- Beginning of an element
- End of an element
- CDATA blocks

You can then define handler functions for these
elements and use them to transform the XML into
something else, for instance Hypertext Markup Language (HTML). Listing 8.1 shows this and outputs the
contents of the XML file as a bulleted HTML list, as
shown in Figure 8.1. The function xml_set_element_
handler() sets the handlers for the beginning and end
of an element, whereas xml_set_character_data_
handler() sets the handler for CDATA blocks. With
xml_parser_set_option(), you can configure the handler, for instance to ignore whitespace and to handle
tag names as case sensitive (then tag names are not
converted into uppercase letters automatically).
The following code contains the code for the handler
functions:

```
function sax_start($sax, $tag, $attr) {
  if ($tag == 'quotes') {
    echo '<ul>';
  } elseif ($tag == 'quote') {
    echo '<li>' . htmlspecialchars($attr['year']) .
      ': ';
  } elseif ($tag == 'phrase') {
    echo '"';
  } elseif ($tag == 'author') {
    echo ' (';
  }
}
function sax_end($sax, $tag) {
```

```
  if ($tag == 'quotes') {
    echo '</ul>';
  } elseif ($tag == 'quote') {
    echo '</li>';
  } elseif ($tag == 'phrase') {
    echo '"';
  } elseif ($tag == 'author') {
    echo ') ';
  }
}
function sax_cdata($sax, $data) {
  echo htmlspecialchars($data);
}
```

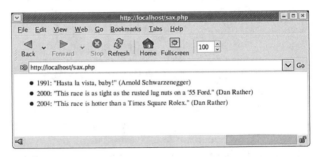

Figure 8.1 HTML created from XML.

NOTE

PHP 5.1 comes with XMLReader included by default. This is a wrapper on libxml2 and mimics the application programming interface (API) of the .NET component for reading XML, XmlTextReader. It is much faster than SAX and just easier to use. As of this writing, it is not very stable yet, but looks quite promising. Not part of the standard PHP 5.1 distribution, but available in PECL, is the associate module XMLWriter that allows write access to XML. More information about both modules is available in a presentation by their author at http://php5.bitflux.org/xmloncrack/.

Using DOM in PHP 4 to Read XML

`domxml_open_mem(file_get_contents('quotes.xml'))`

The W3C's Document Object Model (DOM) defines a unified way to access elements in an XML structure. Therefore, accessing elements in an HTML page using JavaScript's DOM access and accessing elements in an XML file using PHP's DOM access are quite similar.

```php
<?php
  $dom =
  domxml_open_mem(file_get_contents('quotes.xml'));
  echo '<ul>';
  foreach ($dom->get_elements_by_tagname('quote') as
    $element) {
    $attr = $element->attributes();
    $year = htmlspecialchars($attr[0]->value);
    foreach ($element->child_nodes() as $e) {
      if (isset($e->tagname)) {
        if ($e->tagname == 'phrase') {
          $node = $e->first_child();
          $phrase = htmlspecialchars
            ($node->node_value());
        } elseif ($e->tagname == 'author') {
          $node = $e->first_child();
          $author =
          htmlspecialchars($node->node_value());
        }
      }
    }
    echo "<li>$author: \"$phrase\" ($year)</li>";
  }
  echo '</ul>';
?>
```

Parsing XML with DOM (dom-read4.php)

Unfortunately, if you use PHP 4, be aware that the DOM access changed between versions and is not that stable on some systems. Windows users have to use `extension=php_domxml.dll` in `php.ini` and may have to copy `iconv.dll` in the Windows `system32` folder. Other systems have to reconfigure PHP using `–with-dom=/path/to/libxml`. Then `domxml_open_file()` opens a file—using the absolute path! A more portable way is to use `domxml_open_mem` that reads in a string. The return value of both functions offers access to the two methods `get_elements_by_tagname()` and `get_element_by_id()` that return all nodes with a certain tag name or a specific element identified by its ID. Then each node exposes some methods such as the following:

- `first_child()`—First child node
- `last_child()`—Last child node
- `next_sibling()`—Next node
- `previous_sibling()`—Previous node
- `node_value()`—Value of the node

The preceding code uses DOM to access all quotes in the XML file and outputs them.

Using DOM in PHP 5 to Read XML

If you use PHP 5, the main advantage is that libxml2 is used, a much better library than libxml. It is bundled with PHP, so no installation is required. However, the API has changed drastically. First, you instantiate a `DOMDocument` object, then you `load()` a file or `loadXML()` a string. All method names have changed to studly caps, and all properties are real properties, not methods like in PHP 4. The preceding code does the same as the code in the previous phrase, but works under PHP 5.

```php
<?php
  $dom = new DOMDocument();
  $dom->load('quotes.xml');
  echo '<ul>';
  foreach ($dom->getElementsByTagname('quote') as
    $element) {
    $year = $element->getAttribute('year');
    foreach (($element->childNodes) as $e) {
      if (is_a($e, 'DOMElement')) {
        if ($e->tagName == 'phrase') {
          $phrase = htmlspecialchars($e-
            >textContent);
        } elseif ($e->tagName == 'author') {
          $author = htmlspecialchars($e-
            >textContent);
        }
      }
    }
    echo "<li>$author: \"$phrase\" ($year)</li>";
  }
  echo '</ul>';
?>
```

Parsing XML with DOM (dom-read5.php)

Note that the listings use is_a() so that the tag names are only evaluated in nodes of the type DOMElement. This is because whitespace is considered as a DOM node (however, of type DOMText).

> **TIP**
>
> Although the DOM implementations of PHP 4 and PHP 5 are not compatible to each other, they are quite similar. At http://alexandre.alapetite.net/doc-alex/ domxml-php4-php5/, you will find a wrapper that promises to make a PHP 4 DOM script compatible to a PHP 5 DOM.

Using DOM in PHP 4 to Write XML

```
domxml_open_mem(file_get_contents('quotes.xml'))
```

Apart from the read access, it is also possible to build complete XML documents from the ground up using PHP's DOM support. This might look a bit clumsy; however, it works very well when you have to automatically parse a lot of data.

When using PHP 4, the `create_element()` method creates a new element. You can set its content with `set_content()` and attributes with `set_attribute()`. Finally, you access the root element of the XML file with `document_element()` and then call `append_child()`. Finally, `dump_mem()` returns the whole XML file as a string so that you can save it to the hard disk—or you can use `dump_file()` to let PHP do the saving. However, note that `dump_file()` uses an absolute path, so you might be better off with PHP's own file-handling functions.

```php
<?php
  require_once 'stripFormSlashes.inc.php';
  $dom = domxml_open_mem(file_get_contents
    ('quotes.xml'));
  $quote = $dom->create_element('quote');
  $quote->set_attribute('year', $_POST['year']);
  $phrase = $dom->create_element('phrase');
  $phrase->set_content($_POST['quote']);
  $author = $dom->create_element('author');
  $author->set_content($_POST['author']);
  $quote->append_child($phrase);
  $quote->append_child($author);
  $root = $dom->document_element();
  $root->append_child($quote);
  file_put_contents('quotes.xml', $dom->dump_mem());
  echo 'Quote saved.';
?>
```

Creating XML with DOM (dom-write4.php; excerpt)

The preceding code saves author, quote, and year in an XML document, appending to the data already there.

Using DOM in PHP 5 to Write XML

```php
$dom = new DOMDocument();
```

When using PHP 5, the code changes a bit, but most of it is changing to studly caps.

```php
<?php
  require_once 'stripFormSlashes.inc.php';
  $dom = new DOMDocument();
  $dom->load('quotes.xml');
```

```
  $quote = $dom->createElement('quote');
  $quote->setAttribute('year', $_POST['year']);
  $phrase = $dom->createElement('phrase');
  $phraseText = $dom->
createTextNode($_POST['quote']);
  $phrase->appendChild($phraseText);
  $author = $dom->createElement('author');
  $authorText = $dom->
createTextNode($_POST['author']);
  $author->appendChild($authorText);
  $quote->appendChild($phrase);
  $quote->appendChild($author);
  $dom->documentElement->appendChild($quote);
  $dom->save('quotes.xml');
  echo 'Quote saved.';
?>
```

Creating XML with DOM (dom-write5.php; excerpt)

NOTE

PHP 5's DOM extension does not offer something like PHP 5's set_content(), so you have to define the text values of the nodes using the createTextNode() method, as shown in the preceding code.

Using SimpleXML

```
$xml = simplexml_load_file('quotes.xml');
```

One of the greatest new features in PHP 5.1 is the SimpleXML extension, an idea borrowed from a Perl module in CPAN. The approach is as simple as it is ingenious. The most intuitive way to access XML is probably via an object-oriented programming (OOP) approach: Subnodes are properties of their parent nodes/objects, and XML attributes turn into object attributes. This makes accessing XML very easy, including full iterator support, so foreach can be used.

```php
<?php
  $xml = simplexml_load_file('quotes.xml');
  echo '<ul>';
  foreach ($xml->quote as $quote) {
    $year = htmlspecialchars($quote['year']);
    $phrase = htmlspecialchars($quote->phrase);
    $author = htmlspecialchars($quote->author);
    echo "<li>$author: \"$phrase\" ($year)</li>";
  }
  echo '</ul>';
?>
```

Parsing XML with SimpleXML (simplexml-read.php)

This code loads a file using simplexml_load_file()—you can also use simplexml_load_string() for strings—and then reads all information in.

Compare this to the DOM approach. SimpleXML may be slower in some instances than DOM, but the coding is so much quicker.

NOTE

Writing can be done easily, as well. However, it is not possible to append elements without any external help, for instance by using DOM and loading this DOM into SimpleXML using simplexml_import_dom().

Transforming XML with XSL and PHP 4

```
$result = $xslt->process($dom);
echo $xslt->result_dump_mem($result);
```

To use XSL Transformations (XSLT) with PHP, you again have to decide first which PHP version to use. If it's PHP 4, you have to use `extension=php_xslt.dll` in `php.ini` (Windows), or install Sablotron from http://www.gingerall.com/ and use the configuration switches `-enable-xslt -with-xslt-sablot` (for other systems).

```
<?php
  $dom =
domxml_open_mem(file_get_contents('quotes.xml'));
  $xslt = domxml_xslt_stylesheet(
file_get_contents('quotes.xsl'));
  $result = $xslt->process($dom);
  echo $xslt->result_dump_mem($result);
?>
```

Using XSLT with PHP 4 (xslt4.php)

Doing the transformation is a number of four easy steps: Load the XML; load the XSLT; execute the transformation; and, finally, save the result. The preceding phrase contains the code for these steps; the file `quotes.xsl` in the download repository contains markup that transforms the quotes' XML into the well-known HTML bulleted list.

Transforming XML with XSL and PHP 5

```
$result = $xslt->transformToDoc($xml);
echo $result->saveXML();
```

On PHP 5, XSLT is done by libxslt and can be enabled using php_xsl.dll (in php.ini) on Windows and the switch –with-xsl on other platforms. The approach is a bit different: Load both the XML and the XSLT (which is an XML document, as well) into a DOM object, then instantiate an XsltProcessor object. Call importStylesheet() and then transformToDoc().

```php
<?php
  $xml = new DOMDocument();
  $xml->load('quotes.xml');
  $xsl = new DOMDocument();
  $xsl->load('quotes.xsl');
  $xslt = new XsltProcessor();
  $xslt->importStylesheet($xsl);
  $result = $xslt->transformToDoc($xml);
  echo $result->saveXML();
?>
```

Using XSLT with PHP 5 (xslt5.php)

USING XML

TIP

Once again, there is a script that makes the two incompatible XSLT implementations compatible with each other. You find it at http://alexandre.alapetite.net/doc-alex/xslt-php4-php5/.

Validating XML

```
$dom->relaxNGValidate('quotes.rng')
```

PHP 5 can validate XML against three types of files: Document Type Definitions (DTDs), Schemas (.xsd), and relaxNG. For the latter two, the following four methods of the DOM object exist:

- schemaValidate('file.xsd')—Validates against a Schema file

- schemaValidateSource('...')—Validates against a Schema string

- relaxNGValidate('file.rng')—Validates against a relaxNG file

- relaxNGValidateSource('...')—Validates against a relaxNG string

The preceding code uses relaxNGValidate() to validate a (well-formed) XML file against a nonmatching relaxNG file. If you change <element name="person"> to <element name="author"> in the file quotes.rng, the validation succeeds.

```
<?php
  $dom = new DOMDocument;
  $dom->load('quotes.xml');
  echo 'Validation ' .
    (($dom->relaxNGValidate('quotes.rng')) ?
'succeeded.' : 'failed.');
?>
```

Validating XML Against relaxNG (validate-rng.php)

TIP

Creating a relaxNG file can be quite difficult; the Java tool Trang, available at http://thaiopensource.com/relaxng/trang.html, can read in an XML file and create a relaxNG, Schema, or DTD file out of it.

Validating a Schema is similar and shown in the file validate-xsd.php in the download repository. When it comes to validating DTDs, you have to patch the XML a bit. The DTD file must be included in the file or referenced like this:

```
<!DOCTYPE note SYSTEM "quotes.dtd">
```

Then, just load the XML document into a DOM object and call validate(). The following contains the appropriate code; the file referenced in the code repository contains an intentional error in the DTD (month instead of year).

```php
<?php
  $dom = new DOMDocument();
  $dom->load('quotes-dtd.xml');
  echo 'Validation ' .
    (($dom->validate()) ? 'succeeded.' : 'failed.');
?>
```

Validating XML Against a DTD (validate-dtd.php)

What Does PEAR Offer?

As of this writing, the XML section of PEAR contains 28 packages, too many to mention. Here are some of them:

- XML_Beautifier formats XML documents so that they are prettier
- XML_DTD allows parsing of DTDs, even with PHP 4
- XML_Serializer converts XML files into data structures and vice versa
- XML_Util contains a wealth of helper functions for working with XML

Communicating with Others

Most of the previous phrases worked within the ecosystem of the PHP script and the web server in use. However, because some phrases can also be understood by others, this chapter covers some examples of this type. You can connect to remote servers in a variety of ways.

Connecting with HTTP Servers

```
<xmp>
<?php
  echo file_get_contents('http://www.php.net/');
?>
</xmp>
```

Hypertext Transfer Protocol (HTTP) is probably the protocol most often used from PHP to connect with others (apart from various database protocols). Starting with PHP 4.3, it is really easy to connect to such data sources because PHP's stream support was vastly improved in that version (of course, using HTTP in the way this code shows was already possible in earlier PHP releases). The idea is that when you use a file operation, you access a stream of data. In practice, it doesn't really matter whether it's a file on the local system, on a network share, or on a remote server connected via either HTTP, File Transfer Protocol (FTP), or any other supported protocol. Just provide the appropriate filename, and PHP takes care of the rest. The preceding code shows this: It opens the PHP home page and prints its Hypertext Markup Language (HTML) code in the browser. With just one line of code, it cannot get much more simple. Figure 9.1 contains the output.

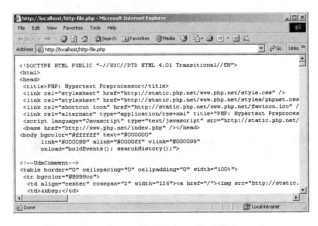

Figure 9.1   A one-liner prints the HTML markup of the PHP home page.

If you want to control the HTTP request by yourself, you can do so by using sockets. First, open a socket with fsockopen() to the web server, and if that works, then send a well-formed HTTP request. The following code implements this again for querying the PHP home page.

```php
<?php
  $fp = @fsockopen('www.php.net', 80, $errno,
    $errstr, 30);
  if ($fp) {
    echo '<xmp>';
    $request = "GET / HTTP/1.0\r\n";
    $request .= "Host: www.php.net\r\n";
    $request .= "Connection: Close\r\n\r\n";
    fwrite($fp, $request);
    while (!feof($fp)) {
      echo fgets($fp, 1024);
    }
    fclose($fp);
    echo '</xmp>';
  } else {
    echo "Error: $errstr (#$errno)";
  }
?>
```

Reading in an HTTP resource using sockets (http-socket.php)

The output is the same, with one difference: The socket approach also returns all HTTP headers sent by the server, whereas the stream wrappers omit them.

> **NOTE**
>
> When it is required to work with HTTP Secure (HTTPS) resources (websites secured with SSL—Secure Sockets Layer), the two approaches still work, although with slight modification:
>
> - When using file functions such as file_get_contents(), just provide an https:// uniform resource locator (URL).
> - When using sockets, use an ssl:// URL.

Connecting with FTP Servers

```
file_get_contents('ftp://ftp.leo.org/.mnt/0/
mirrors/apache/httpd/README.html')
```

When accessing FTP servers, PHP's stream wrappers come in very handy, as well. You only have read access, but the access is binary-safe nonetheless. This code shows how to download the current README file for Apache from an FTP server and save it to the local hard disk using file_get_contents(). Writing is also possible; just use file_put_contents() or the correct file mode for fopen(). Note, though, that both reading and writing simultaneously is not yet supported.

```php
<?php
  $data =
file_get_contents('ftp://ftp.leo.org/.mnt/0/
  mirrors/apache/httpd/README.html');
  file_put_contents('Apache-README.html', $data);
  echo 'File written.';
?>
```

Reading in an FTP file (ftp-file.php; excerpt)

TIP

If you do not provide any credentials, PHP tries to log you in to the FTP server using a guest account most public FTP servers offer. You can, however, also provide the credentials yourself:

```
$data = file_get_contents
  ('ftp://USER:PASSWORD@ftp.example.com/');
```

This works for HTTP resources (see previous phrase), too!

PHP also comes with built-in support for FTP and a special set of functions that implement the complete FTP functionality defined in the associated Request for Comment (RFC). In the Windows distributions, this is enabled by default, whereas on other systems, PHP has to be configured with the switch – enable-ftp. Then, using the FTP server usually consists of the following steps:

- Connect to the server using ftp_connect()
- Log in using ftp_login()
- Go to the target directory using ftp_chdir()

- Read a file—ftp_get()—from or write a file—ftp_put()—to the FTP server

- Close the connection using ftp_close()

Because reading probably is more common than writing, the following shows the former task being executed. Again, the Apache README is fetched from an FTP server.

```php
<?php
  $ftp = @ftp_connect('ftp.leo.org');
  $login = @ftp_login($ftp, 'anonymous',
    'email@example.com');
  if ($ftp && $login) {
    ftp_chdir($ftp, '/.mnt/0/mirrors/apache/
      httpd/');
    ftp_get($ftp, 'Apache-README-ftp.html',
      'README.html', FTP_ASCII);
    echo 'File written.';
    ftp_close($ftp);
  } else {
    echo 'Error!';
  }
?>
```

Reading in an FTP file using the built-in functions (ftp-functions.php)

Note that the syntax of ftp_get() is a bit strange. After the FTP resource, you have to provide first the local filename, then the remote filename (intuitively, you would expect it to be the other way around). The last parameter is the transfer mode: FTP_ASCII for text files and FTP_BINARY for all other data.

Checking Whether a Server Is Still Reacting

Assume you have a web server and you want to check periodically if it didn't crash again. Then, using a PHP script for this task can be a good idea. Just open a socket to the server and wait (the last parameter of fsockopen() is a timeout value). After this time has elapsed, you know if the server is online or offline.

```php
<?php
  $server = 'localhost';
  $port = '80';
  $status = 'unavailable';
  $fp = @fsockopen($server, $port, $errno, $errstr,
    10);
  if ($fp) {
    $status = 'alive, but not responding';
    fwrite($fp, "HEAD / HTTP/1.0\r\n");
    fwrite($fp, "Host: $server:$port\r\n\r\n");
    if (strlen(@fread($fp, 1024)) > 0) {
      $status = 'alive and kicking';
    }
    fclose($fp);
  }
  echo "The server is $status.";
?>
```

Checking the status of a server (serverstatus.php)

COMMUNICATING WITH OTHERS

TIP

This works well if only one server's status must be checked. If there are several servers, this approach has some disadvantages. The call to fsockopen() might take up to the timeout value until the next command is executed. Therefore, all servers are checked sequentially and synchronously. This just takes too long for several servers. However, with PHP 5 and stream sockets, this can be done asynchronously. The code is a bit complicated, but Wez Furlong explains this approach in great detail at http://netevil.org/node.php?nid=280.

Understanding Web Services

Some people say Web Services are just old wine in new bottles because the idea behind them is far from new. The basic principle is: Two machines talk to each other. For instance, one machine contains some business logic or, more generally, some information, and the other machine requests this information (or wants to use the business logic).

This has been done for many years, but only a few years ago the major players sat together and started to work on protocols to put the whole communication on top of standards. Some of these standards are now under the aegis of the World Wide Web Consortium (W3C), whereas others are managed by the Organization for the Advancement of Structured Information Standards (OASIS) consortium.

A multitude of books are available on Web Services, with quite a lot of pages. However, in accordance with the concept of this phrasebook, this chapter puts it simple but still gives you all you need to know. There is a protocol that is used to transfer both the request to the Web Service and its response. There are several possiblities, but these two are most common:

- XML-RPC stands for Remote Procedure Call and uses a very simple XML dialect to transport function calls, parameters, and return values. This approach is sometimes called REST, for Representational State. There are some fierce debates about which is better, this protocol or the next one. To make a short and ugly story short: Both have advantages (and disadvantages).

- SOAP once stood for Simple Object Access Protocol, but because it is neither simple nor has too much to do with object access, today SOAP just stands for ... SOAP. It is a rather complex protocol but overcomes many of the limitations of XML-RPC (which was, by the way, created by some parties who also worked on SOAP).

Most of the time, XML-RPC or SOAP calls are transported via HTTP as the carrier protocol. However, other protocols are also possible, including Simple Mail Transfer Protocol (SMTP) or even User Datagram Protocol (UDP).

There is one more important aspect when using SOAP. When you know exactly how a Web Service is implemented, you also know how to call (access, or consume) it. However, many times this information is not available, so there must be a kind of self-description of the Web Service that contains all relevant information, such as which methods or functions are exposed, which parameters and data types do they expect, and what they return. This can be done using a specifically crafted XML file, as well. The standard behind that is Web Services Description Language

(WSDL). Today, WSDL is used for all relevant Web Services because then using them is quite simple. Most server-side technologies offer one (or more) means to just read in the WSDL and then access the Web Service like you would access a locally available class.

Generating all this XML is quite complicated. Not that PHP doesn't have good XML support, but the syntax can be quite hard. Luckily, some extensions and external packages make using Web Services much easier. The following phrases each implement a Web Service that just adds two numbers. You will certainly be more imaginative and create some real-world Web Services, based upon this information.

Creating a Web Service with PEAR::XML-RPC

Several XML-RPC implementations are out there, but the one most widely used and also in active development is PEAR::XML-RPC, available at http://pear.php.net/package/XML_RPC/. It is a PEAR port of another XML-RPC library and adds some fixes that didn't make it in the original distribution. You can install it with `pear upgrade XML_RPC`, to get the latest and greatest version.

To provide such a Web Service, you have to instantiate the `XML_RPC_Server` class and provide some information about the service: which function to use, its description, and, of course, the signature (which parameter types are passed, which data type is returned). The preceding code contains this information for a simple "add two numbers" Web Service.

```php
<?php
  require_once 'XML/RPC/Server.php';

  $description = 'adds two numbers';
  $signature = array(
    array('int', 'int', 'int')
  );

  $xmlrpc = new XML_RPC_Server(
    array('phrasebook.php.add' =>
      array(
        'function' => 'add',
        'docstring' => $description,
        'signature' => $signature
      )
    )
  );
?>
```

Information about the XML-RPC Web Service
(xmlrpc-pear-server.php; excerpt)

Note that the signature contains the data types of all input parameters plus the data type of the return value; that's why 'int' appears three times and not just twice.

Now the only thing missing is the actual business logic, the function to add. This is a bit tricky: First, the getParam() method returns all parameters provided to the function; then, the scalarval() retrieves the actual value of such a parameter. Then, the actual adding of the numbers can be done, by returning a suitable XML_RPC_Response object. For instance:

```php
function add($params) {
  $a = $params->getParam(0);
  $b = $params->getParam(1);
  if (isset($a) && isset($b)) {
```

```php
    if ($a->scalartyp() == 'int' && $b->scalartyp()
      == 'int') {
      $a = $a->scalarval();
      $b = $b->scalarval();
      $c = new XML_RPC_Value($a + $b, 'int');
      return new XML_RPC_Response($c);
    } else {
      global $XML_RPC_erruser;
      return new XML_RPC_Response(0,
        $XML_RPC_erruser,
        'wrong parameters');
    }
  }
}
```

Consuming a Web Service with PEAR::XML-RPC

Querying the Web Service is rather easy. Just instanti-ate the XML_RPC_Client class (providing name, server, and port of the service), then craft a message with all the parameters, and finally send this message to the server. You receive the result of the Web Service call in return—or an error message. The code calls the Web Services from the previous phrase, assuming that it is accessible using http://localhost/ xlmrpc-pear-server.php on port 80.

```php
<?php
  require_once 'XML/RPC.php';

  $a = 47;
  $b = 11;

  $xmlrpc = new XML_RPC_Client(
```

```php
  '/xmlrpc-pear-server.php',
  'localhost',
  80
);

$msg = new XML_RPC_Message(
  'phrasebook.php.add',
  array(
    new XML_RPC_Value($a, 'int'),
    new XML_RPC_Value($b, 'int')
  )
);

$response = $xmlrpc->send($msg);
$result = $response->value();
if (!$response->faultCode()) {
  echo "$a + $b = " . $result->scalarval();
} else {
  echo 'Error #' . $response->faultCode() . ': ' .
    $response->faultString();
}
?>
```

Calling an XML-RPC Web Service (xmlrpc-pear-client.php)

COMMUNICATING WITH OTHERS

TIP

When you call $xmlrpc->setDebug(1), debugging messages are turned on, making it easier for you to find out what is going wrong.

NOTE

For PHP 5 only, a new extension is available, called XMLRPCi (the i stands for improved), that uses libxml2 for the XML-RPC calls. However, there has only been one release yet, with very minimal documentation, so it is hardly in use at the moment.

Creating a Web Service with NuSOAP

At http://dietrich.ganx4.com/nusoap/ and http://sourceforge.net/projects/nusoap/, you will find NuSOAP, one of the best-known SOAP classes for PHP. Some might even know its predecessor, SOAPx4. For some time, releases weren't done very often, but now the project is active again. Nevertheless, you might be better off to check the Concurrent Versions System (CVS) system for the most recent code. Even though you might find several files there, nusoap.php is the one you want.

```php
<?php
  require_once 'nusoap.php';

  $soap = new soap_server;
  $soap->register('add');
  $soap->service($HTTP_RAW_POST_DATA);

  function add($a, $b) {
    return $a + $b;
  }
?>
```

Calling an XML-RPC Web Service (xmlrpc-pear-client.php)

NOTE
As of this writing, NuSOAP only works under PHP 4, but a PHP 5 port is rumored to be under way.

Creating a Web Service with NuSOAP is really simple because the module takes care of all the painful things, including SOAP. Just follow these steps:

1. Write the function you want to expose as a web method

2. Instantiate the `soap_server` class

3. Register your function with the SOAP server

4. Call the `service()` method and submit `$HTTP_RAW_POST_DATA` as the parameter

This code implements a SOAP server using NuSOAP. Figure 9.2 shows the output in the browser when you are trying to call the Web Service directly from the client. The error message says that the XML was empty—of course, because we didn't send a request!

Automatically Generating WSDL with NuSOAP

As mentioned previously, current Web Services do almost always use WSDL. Writing WSDL manually is a real pain and very error-prone, but most serious Web Services implementations for PHP can create WSDL automatically. However, because PHP is no strongly typed language, they need some help.

To do so with NuSOAP, the code from the previous section must be expanded a bit. First, a method `configureWSDL()` must be called to provide the name and the namespace of the service. Then, the signature of the method must be provided (which parameters go in, which go out). Then, the server is started. However, this time whether `$HTTP_RAW_POST_DATA` is set is checked or not. This is because when it is not set, the user has made a GET request, so there might be a chance that he just wants the WSDL description.

```php
<?php
  require_once 'nusoap.php';

  $soap = new soap_server;
  $soap->configureWSDL('AddService', 'http://php.
    phrasebook.org/');
  $soap->wsdl->schemaTargetNamespace = 'http://
    soapinterop.org/xsd/';
  $soap->register(
    'add',
    array('a' => 'xsd:int', 'b' => 'xsd:int'),
    array('c' => 'xsd:int'),
    'http://soapinterop.org/'
  );
  $soap->service(isset($HTTP_RAW_POST_DATA) ?
    $HTTP_RAW_POST_DATA : '');

  function add($a, $b) {
    return $a + $b;
  }
?>
```

A WSDL-enabled Web Service with NuSOAP (wsdl-nusoap-server.php)

Back to the WSDL: Figure 9.3 shows the Web Service in the browser when called using GET. A click on the link shows some information about the add() method. In Figure 9.4, you see what happens when you append ?WSDL to the URL of the script (or click on the WSDL link): The WSDL for the service is automatically generated. Imagine if you had to do this manually...

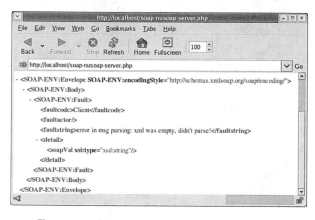

Figure 9.2   This error message is a good sign—the
script seems to work (so far).

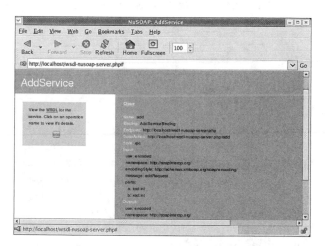

Figure 9.3   Now NuSOAP automatically generates an
info page for the service.

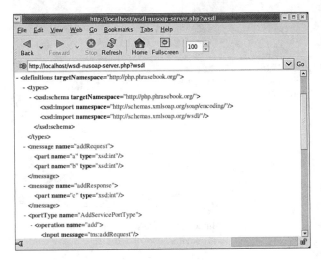

Figure 9.4 This WSDL is generated by NuSOAP, not by the programmer.

Consuming a Web Service with NuSOAP

Actually, using a NuSOAP service is even easier than creating one. You just have to load the WSDL file and then get a so-called proxy class: That's a local class that behaves just as if the Web Service is a local class, too. So, you can call the Web Service's methods directly, and NuSOAP takes care of all the rest (including opening a connection to the remote server, assembling and parsing XML, and so on).

To do this, the soapclient class (without the under-score character) must be instantiated, and then the getProxy() method creates the proxy class. The code implements this for the demo service from the previous example. Note the URL of the WSDL file: It's the Web Service's URL plus ?wsdl appended to the end; change the URL accordingly for your system.

```php
<?php
  require_once 'nusoap.php';

  $soap = new soapclient('http://localhost/
    wsdl-nusoap-server.php?wsdl', true);
  $proxy = $soap->getProxy();
  $result = $proxy->add(47, 11);
  echo "47 + 11 = $result";
?>
```

Consuming the Web Service with NuSOAP (wsdl-nusoap-client.php)

NOTE

Appending ?wsdl to the URL to get the WSDL description of a Web Service is an idea borrowed from Microsoft .NET. However, there the appendix is not case sensitive, whereas NuSOAP requires it to be in lowercase letters. Keep this in mind when working cross-platform.

WARNING

On some systems, NuSOAP has problems when PHP is configured as a common gateway interface (CGI), not as a module built in to the web server. You then see strange paths in the WSDL file.

COMMUNICATING WITH OTHERS

Creating a Web Service with PEAR::SOAP

In PHP's official package repository PEAR, you can find a SOAP extension at http://pear.php.net/ package/SOAP. It depends on several other packages, so you do need to install all that are mentioned on the download page. The current released version works under PHP 4, but the CVS system of PHP (browsable online via http://cvs.php.net/) contains a port for PHP 5. This book uses the PHP 4 version that seems to be more tested and in use than the PHP 5 version from CVS. Use pear install -f SOAP; you might get a list of packages that are required for PEAR::SOAP to run.

```php
<?php
  error_reporting(E_ALL ^ E_NOTICE);
  require_once 'SOAP/Server.php';

  $soap = new SOAP_Server;
  $service = new ServiceClass();
  $soap->addObjectMap($service, 'urn:php-phrasebook-
    soapservice');
  $soap->service($HTTP_RAW_POST_DATA);

  class ServiceClass {
    function add($a, $b) {
      return $a + $b;
    }
  }
?>
```

A Web Service with PEAR::SOAP (soap-pear-server.php)

Providing a Web Service is again a matter of a few lines of code: Instantiate a class (SOAP_Server), and then attach the business logic to it (this time, by putting it into a class and then instantiating the class). Finally, call addObjectMap() to provide a uniform resource name (URN) for the method and then connect it with the method service() to $HTTP_RAW_POST_DATA. This code contains all the details, so you can start from there for your own Web Service.

> **WARNING**
> Unfortunately, PEAR::SOAP currently does not work when error_reporting is set to E_ALL because notices occur in the code. Therefore, the code in this phrase sets the error reporting to a less severe value before loading the PEAR::SOAP classes.

Automatically Generating WSDL with PEAR::SOAP

PEAR::SOAP can also automatically create WSDL; however, it needs some assistance by the programmer. First, the constructor of the Web Service's class must set a __dispatch_map property that contains a list of input and output parameters. The __dispatch_map property is an array (therefore, several operations per Web Service are supported), and the name of the function is the key for the signature.

Also, you need some code that checks the URL. If ?wsdl is appended, the WSDL must be returned by the service. For this, the SOAP_DISCO_Server class is instantiated and then its method getWSDL() gets called.

```
class ServiceClass {
  var $__dispatch_map = array();

  function ServiceClass() {
    $this->__dispatch_map['add'] = array(
      'in'  => array('a' => 'int', 'b' => 'int'),
      'out' => array('c' => 'int')
    );
  }

  function __dispatch($method) {
    if (isset($this->__dispatch_map[$method])) {
      return $this->__dispatch_map[$method];
    } else {
      return null;
    }
  }
  ..
}
```

A WSDL-enabled Web Service with NuSOAP
(wsdl-nusoap-server.php; excerpt)

The following contains the rest of the code for
the server; as you would expect, calling the URL
with ?wsdl at the end creates the service's WSDL
description.

```
<?php
  error_reporting(E_ALL ^ E_NOTICE);
  require_once 'SOAP/Server.php';

  $soap = new SOAP_Server;
  $service = new ServiceClass();
  $soap->addObjectMap($service, 'urn:php-phrasebook-
    soapservice');
```

```php
  if (isset($_SERVER['REQUEST_METHOD']) &&
    $_SERVER['REQUEST_METHOD'] == 'POST') {
    $soap->service($HTTP_RAW_POST_DATA);
  } else {
    require_once 'SOAP/Disco.php';
    $disco = new SOAP_DISCO_Server($soap,
      'DiscoServer');
    if (isset($_SERVER['QUERY_STRING']) &&
      strpos($_SERVER['QUERY_STRING'], 'wsdl') ===
        0) {
      header('Content-type: text/xml');
      echo $disco->getWSDL();
    }
  }

  class ServiceClass {
    // ...
  }
?>
```

Consuming a Web Service with PEAR::SOAP

After the Web Service is created and does offer WSDL generation, a proxy class is very easy to get, thanks to PEAR::SOAP. Instantiate the SOAP_WSDL class with the WSDL description, call getProxy(), and then use the proxy. This is very short but does quite a lot of SOAP in the background.

COMMUNICATING WITH OTHERS

```php
<?php
  error_reporting(E_ALL ^ E_NOTICE);
  require_once 'SOAP/Client.php';

  $soap = new SOAP_WSDL('http://localhost/
    wsdl-pear-server.php?wsdl');
  $proxy = $soap->getProxy();
  $result = $proxy->add(47, 11);
  if (PEAR::isError($result)) {
    echo $result->getMessage();
  } else {
    echo "47 + 11 = $result";
  }
?>
```

Consuming the Web Service with PEAR::SOAP (wsdl-pear-client.php)

Creating a Web Service with PHP 5's SOAP Extension

One of the key features of PHP 5 is the new SOAP extension. Because it is written in C, it is much faster than anything that is coded in PHP alone. However, the extension is relatively new, so there are still some hiccups and missing features. However, it works well on many occasions.

You have to configure PHP with –enable-soap to use the extension; Windows users have to add extension=php_soap.dll to their php.ini configuration file. Then, the extension is available and writing a SOAP server is quite easy.

Again, it's a small number of steps: Instantiate the SoapServer class, add your function with addFunction(), and, finally, call handle().

```php
<?php
  $soap = new SoapServer(null, array('uri' =>
    'http://php.phrasebook.org/'));
  $soap->addFunction('add');
  $soap->handle();

  function add($a, $b) {
    return $a + $b;
  }
?>
```

A Web Service with PHP5-SOAP (soap-php5-server.php)

TIP

PHP 5-SOAP originated as a PECL extension. So, it is also possible to use this extension under PHP 4, just grab the code from CVS. However, no precompiled Windows binaries are available at the moment, and chances are that there never will be any.

COMMUNICATING WITH OTHERS

Automatically Generating WSDL with PHP 5's SOAP Extension

The greatest shortcoming of PHP5-SOAP is that there is no way to automatically generate WSDL with it. This is not often mentioned; however, it does create problems in real life. WSDL is so complicated that errors in the WSDL are hard to see and even harder to find.

However, you can create such a WSDL description for a Web Service in several ways, most of which have been used in real-world projects:

- Use NuSOAP or PEAR::SOAP to create a similar service, just to get the WSDL—just change the `<soap:address>` element
- Use the class Ctrx_SOAP_AutoDiscover (available at http://crtx.org/index.php?area=Main&page=CrtxSoapAutoDiscover)
- Use the Webservice Helper tool (available at http://www.jool.nl/new/index.php?file_id=1)
- Use the WSDL_Gen class (available at http://www.schlossnagle.org/~george/php/WSDL_Gen.tgz)

So as you can see, WSDL support is being worked on, not as part of the SOAP extension itself, but in the form of external projects. But hopes are that this will change some day.

If you finally have a WSDL description of your service (in the download archive, you will find a file `AddService.wsdl` that originated from the PEAR::SOAP–generated WSDL), the code for the server must only be slightly updated. The first parameter for the `SoapServer` instantiation receives the WSDL URL; also, the method(s) of the Web Service must be put in a class. Then, setClass() provides the SOAP extension with the name of the class to be used.

```php
<?php
  $soap = new SoapServer(
    'AddService.wsdl',
    array('uri' => 'http://php.phrasebook.org/')
  );
  $soap->setClass('ServiceClass');
  $soap->handle();

  class ServiceClass {
    function add($a, $b) {
      return $a + $b;
    }
  }
?>
```

Consuming a Web Service with PHP 5's SOAP Extension

Consumption is again easy, as long as you have a WSDL description. This code calls the Web Services and also catches any errors, thanks to PHP 5's try-catch mechanism.

```php
<?php
  $soap = new SoapClient('AddService.wsdl');
  try {
    $result = $soap->add(47, 11);
    echo "47 + 11 = $result";
  } catch (SoapFault $e) {
    echo "Error: {$e->faultstring}";
  }
}
```

Consuming the Web Service with PHP5-SOAP (wsdl-php5-client.php)

> **TIP**
>
> In an attempt to boost performance, PHP 5's SOAP extension defaults to caching WSDL. The following are the standard settings from php.ini-recommended:
>
> ```
> [soap]
> ; Enables or disables WSDL caching feature.
> soap.wsdl_cache_enabled=1
> ; Sets the directory name where SOAP extension
>   will put cache files.
> soap.wsdl_cache_dir="/tmp"
> ; (time to live) Sets the number of seconds
> while cached file will be used
> ; instead of original one.
> soap.wsdl_cache_ttl=86400
> ```
>
> When developing a Web Service and maybe changing the WSDL, this is, of course, a no-brainer. Therefore, set soap.wsdl_cache_enabled to Off during development, but turn it on on production servers.

Using the Worst Acronym Ever: AJAX

Wikipedia lists over a dozen different meanings for the term "Ajax," including a soccer team from the Netherlands, two figures of Homer's *Iliad*, and a house-hold-cleaning product. However, since several months ago, AJAX also stands for "Asynchronous JavaScript + XML." The technology is far from new (the underlying technology, XML HTTP requests from JavaScript, are supported by recent versions of Internet Explorer, and Mozilla browsers including Firefox, Safari, and Konqueror—also, XML is not required at all for this), but only after this really stupid term was coined, did people actually start using it.

The basic principle is that JavaScript is now able to call a remote server and then process its return values, without having to reload the whole page. Of course, this has little to do with PHP; however, some AJAX classes make using AJAX from within PHP very easy.

This final phrase of the book shows a very short demonstration of "AJAX." This phrase uses the Sajax toolkit (the *S* stands for simple) available at http://www.modernmethod.com/sajax/.

The complete code for this example is quite long because both PHP and JavaScript are needed. First, we need the server-side logic. For this, we the Sajax toolkit is loaded, which comes as a single PHP file. We then "export" (register) all PHP functions we want to use from the client-side. The following example has a small function that generates a random RGB color.

COMMUNICATING WITH OTHERS

```php
<?php
  require_once 'Sajax.php';

  sajax_init();
  sajax_export('randomColor');
  sajax_handle_client_request();

  function randomColor() {
    $color = '#';
    for ($i=0; $i<3; $i++) {
      $color .= dechex(rand(0, 255));
    }
    return $color;
  }
?>
```

The server-side part of the application (ajax.php; excerpt)

On the client-side, a call to the (PHP) function
sajax_show_javascript() does most of the work—it
creates some lines of JavaScript code that take care of
the requests to the web server in the background.
Then, all PHP functions that have been registered
before can be called on the client-side by prepending
x_ to the name of the function. As a parameter, you
have to provide the name of a callback function; this
function is then called when the server-side has
responded to the request.

The following code calls the randomColor() PHP function every five seconds and then writes a text in this
random color—all without server round-trips! Figure
9.5 shows the result.

```
<script language="JavaScript" ype="text/javascript"
  ><!--
<?php
  sajax_show_javascript();
?>
  changeColor();
  setInterval('changeColor()', 5000);

  function changeColor() {
    x_randomColor(randomColor_callback);
  }

  function randomColor_callback(result) {
    var text = '<span style="color: ' + result +
      '">What a dumb acronym ...</span>';
    document.getElementById('output').innerHTML =
      text;
  }
//--></script>
...
<div id="output"></div>
```

The client-side part of the application (ajax.php; excerpt)

Figure 9.5 The text appears, using
JavaScript and PHP.

What Does PEAR Offer?

Along with the several modules mentioned in this chapter, the following PEAR packages offer functionality that can be helpful when connecting with others using PHP:

- The HTTP category of PEAR offers some relevant packages, including HTTP, HTTP_Client, HTTP_Header, HTTP_Request, and HTTP_Server.

- Likewise, you can find useful packages in the Networking category, including Net_FTP, Net_IMAP, and Net_Socket.

- The Services category of PEAR contains several classes that offer an easy to use interface for well-known Web Services.

Index

How can we make this index more useful? Email us at indexes@samspublishing.com

B-C

INDEX

How can we make this index more useful? Email us at indexes@samspublishing.com

293

How can we make this index more useful? Email us at indexes@samspublishing.com

295

INDEX

N

O

How can we make this index more useful? Email us at indexes@samspublishing.com

299

Q-R

INDEX

X-Y-Z

INDEX